The Keeper of the Trees

by D. Rodney Blanks

Published by
CSS Publishing

Additional copies available.
Use order form in the back of this book.

Published by CSS Publishing
Ruidoso Downs, New Mexico

First Edition
First Printing • 500 • November, 1996

Library of Congress Catalog Card Number: 96-97121
ISBN 1-57502-326-1

Additional copies of *The Keeper of the Trees* may be obtained by
sending a check for $11.00 (includes postage and handling) to
the address below. For your convenience, an order form can
be found at the back of this book.

CSS Publishing
P.O. Box 779
Ruidoso Downs, NM 88346-0779

The Keeper of the Trees may be obtained by retail outlets
at special rates. Write to the above address for more information.

Printed in the USA by

**3212 E. Hwy 30
Kearney, NE 68847
800-650-7888**

To Syl, my soulmate, who has tolerated my romance with this, my mistress, for the last five years. Without her patience, encouragement, inspiration, and belief in me, this endeavor may have remained a dream unrealized. It is to her that I dedicate this book.

Oxymora

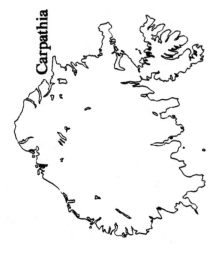

Carpathia

Malthus

Pre-Adamic World

Nod

Oxymora

Chapter 1

The Banishment

For the fifth time in a hundred years, the Flying Star with the Fiery Tail illuminated the Carpathian winter sky and it had grown larger, brighter, nearer with each pass. Many generations had passed since the High Mantis had prophesied the coming of the Great Carom, and the ancient prophecy had been largely ignored or forgotten until the Star appeared, a dot on the western horizon, and began slowly carving its backward path across the night sky. But now, a hundred years later, it was twice the size of the brightest star, and twice the brilliance. Soon it would strike, flinging land and water and living things into endless sky. Everything the descendants of Andon and Fonta had built would be lost to the ages. This world was doomed to die.

No one doubted that cataclysmic destruction was imminent. Even the astronomers conceded that the world was destined to collide with the cursed Star, but no one knew how many more times would it pass, ever closer, before it struck. Each time the Star appeared, it was ushered in by frustration, fear and bewilderment as people were reminded of their impotence, their vulnerability, their mortality. The Year of the Star was a restless year indeed. It was a time when rational thought gave way to self-pity, hopelessness and despair as people tried to cope with the inevitability of their demise.

But Aleph's world had already ended. As he awoke and slowly began to stir from the spot where he had lain throughout the night his muscles quickly yielded to pain. The pain! In all of his twenty years, he had never experienced such pain!

His thoughts suddenly snapped to the events of the night before--the launching party, the great feast celebrating his banishment, the agony and humiliation as they whipped him, beat him and tore at his flesh, his bitter tears as he watched his beloved Carpathia fade into darkness. He could still see their faces, delighted with scornful glee as they lashed his back. He could still hear their cries of righteous indignation as they set him adrift. He could still hear the eerie sound of their revelry drifting across the dark sea as he floated away. And then there had been exhaustion, darkness and merciful oblivion.

Propping himself up on one elbow, Aleph squinted against the blinding morning light. As the sun's rays beat down through the cloudless sky, beads of sweat began to spot his forehead then trickle down his face, stinging his eyes. He prayed for a cool breeze, but nothing would move the muggy stillness. Grasping the side of his tiny craft, he pulled himself slowly up to a sitting position and looked out over the empty sea toward Carpathia.

Suddenly, his vision blurred, his head buzzed, a choking lump rose to his throat. Straining against sore muscles, he hung himself over the side and began retching. When he could heave no more, he lay there, arms dangling in the water, face inches above it. Opening his eyes, he stared into the watery mirror and hardly recognized his own image. There were cuts above his swollen eyes, his cheeks were bruised, his blonde beard was matted with blood. His robes hung loosely in tatters about his shoulders and draped over his tall, thin frame like a rumpled tent. It was the reflection of a man agonized by disappointment and disillusionment.

Though it seemed an eternity ago, only three days had passed since he had been arrested for heresy, two days since he had been tried and convicted by the High Court, one day since he had been marked as an Outlander and banished. All this, and his only crime was following The Way of the Ascetic. The Way had long been scorned by Carpathian society. The Churchwardens saw to that because those who followed The Way did not give the church authority over their religion. But Aleph had no idea to what lengths people would go in the name of goodness.

The shrill screech of a sea gull shattered his ruminations and snapped his focus back to his current predicament. Here he was, floating in a hollowed-out tree with loosely-slatted planks for a deck, a mast made from an old flag standard, and a tattered flag for sail. A canvas-covered bow little larger than a knapsack held his supplies and all his worldly goods. He was in a floating coffin at the mercy of a fickle sea.

Thirsty and hungry, he gathered his faculties and tried to stand, but a searing pain shot through his back and legs sending him sprawling back to the splintery deck. The cuts and welts across his back from the lashing, the bruises on his face and body from fists and stones, the abrasions from ropes which had cut into his wrists and ankles had left him weak, sore, exhausted.

He rolled onto his back and glared at the sky, wishing angrily that the Star would strike now and destroy them all, but the Star was already waning. They would be spared for another twenty years.

His anger soon gave way to regrets and tears began to flow down his cheeks. Maybe the Churchwardens were right after all. They warned of the dangers of following The Way and maybe they were right. For a moment he wished he had never heard of The Way of the Ascetic! He wished he had never doubted the unquestioning obedience the Precepts demanded. Rules, after all, are to be followed.

If anyone knew about rules, it was Aleph. His institutional caretakers at the church orphanage had inundated him with the teachings of the Precepts of Pax since his abandonment there at the age of two. He had tried to follow the Precepts, but the abject obedience they demanded did not return what they promised. Try as he might to have faith, he could never rid himself of his fears, and the pain of the comfort The Precepts offered was just too great to bear.

When he discovered The Way, it was a light in the darkness. It was the only thing he had ever found that accepted him unconditionally, and he wanted more. He knew he risked reprisal from the deeply religious, but the punishment he had received for seeking acceptance was more stern than he had ever imagined. Banishment had been the most degrading, humiliating experience of his young life.

Aleph slumped there on the tiny, weather-grayed deck, defeated. Gut-wrenching sobs soon spilled over the endless sea. He cried until he was exhausted, and with a final heaving sigh, he curled into a ball, hugged himself tightly and slept.

When he awoke, it was mid-afternoon. He stirred slowly, straining against the pain of his injuries. Dragging himself up to the side of his vessel once more, he sat there staring out over the boundless ocean. Suddenly, the danger of his immediate dilemma hit him and his hurt, anger, and regrets switched in an instant to fear and panic. He must set sail for land lest he be swallowed up! Scanning the vast ocean which stretched from horizon to horizon, he considered his options. Far to the northwest lay Malthus, but everyone knew that the Malthusians were welcoming of no one and he quickly dismissed that idea. Beyond Malthus lay Nod, but the distance was so great that he would surely not survive the voyage, for the launching party had only provided him with sufficient rations for thirty days. To the southwest lay a chain of deserted islands and he considered momentarily the life of a hermit. Living all alone on some tropic isle had a certain appeal but the thought of perpetuating his isolation was grim indeed.

Aleph's choice was clear. Despite all foreboding of doom, it was toward the northeast, toward Oxymora, the land of the Ascetic, that he would set sail. He had sacrificed his beloved Carpathia to follow The Way and he was resolved to see if the legends were true. With sheer determination, he gripped the mast with both hands and pulled himself to his feet. He set his eyes toward the northeastern horizon, turned his tiny craft, set his sails and caught a gentle breeze which pushed him steadily toward Oxymora.

Once under way, he settled back into his berth and listened to the waves methodically sloshing by, gently rocking him onward. As he lay there exhausted, gazing into the depth of the sky, he slowly drifted off to sleep, his head swimming with all he knew, all he believed, and all he could imagine about Oxymora and the Ascetic.

For days on the open sea, Aleph clung tightly to his small thread of hope, then on the eighteenth morning he first glimpsed the distant mist-shrouded peak of Mount Erudite. Continuing his northeasterly course, he watched in awe as it rose ominously out of the sea, looming dark and gray above the open waters.

His excitement ran high as the possibility of meeting the Ascetic became a little more real, but neither harbor nor beach welcomed him. From every direction he found only high rock cliffs which rose sharply out of the sea. He dared not venture too close lest he be smashed by powerful waves breaking over the jagged reefs. Oxymora was completely unapproachable and his hopes were momentarily as dashed as were the waves upon the rocks.

By dusk, the jagged rock face of Oxymora's entire southern shore sprawled before him as a great dam which held back the horizon. As darkness slowly swallowed the remaining light, he lowered his sails and fell into his berth, exhausted from the excitement, anticipation, disappointment and frustration the day had held. He let his small vessel drift in the black waters below the cliffs and fell into a deep sleep.

He was awakened at dawn by familiar sounds--birds singing, trees rustling in the breeze, water rushing--sounds he had not expected to hear. Peering over the bow of his vessel, he found himself floating in a tranquil pool surrounded by a narrow sandy beach which gave way to lush greenery. The gentle roar of a nearby waterfall filled his ears, a doe and her fawn were lazily drinking at the edge of the water, trees laden with fruit stood majestically beyond the beach. There was life all around, and in abundance.

Completely lost and confused, he wondered for a moment if he were dreaming, or insane, or even dead and in the Place of Eternal Comfort. Gathering his composure, he focused his attention on getting his feet on solid ground. Looking around cautiously, he rowed eagerly toward the shore. Convinced he was quite alone, he beached his vessel and disembarked. Dropping to his knees, he dug his fingers into the soft sand, then stretched his arms skyward and let go a great bellow.

He explored this lush garden of delights with childlike exuberance, eating the ripe berries, nuts and fruits, and drinking the cool fresh water. When he had taken his fill, the sun was already high overhead. He stretched himself upon the beach to gaze at the sky and contemplate his new world.

He napped into mid-afternoon, when a clap of thunder from dark clouds building overhead startled him awake. Unable to bring himself to return to the vessel where he had spent the last eighteen days, he looked about for alternative shelter. Suddenly, his gaze fell upon an apparently well-traveled path which led into the dense wood, and he scurried up the trail in search of a cave or overhanging rocks which might protect him. At least the umbrella of trees would provide some cover. Lightning struck a tree to his right, and as his attention snapped toward the sharp crack, he saw the small dark mouth of a cave. Weighing the danger which might lie in the cave against the danger of the storm, he bounded over the forest floor past the smoking tree and reached the cave just as a gentle shower began. As he peeked cautiously inside, he found the cave quite inviting. Entering the darkness, he found it no larger than a small house, with solid walls on all sides and a roof which hovered an arm's reach overhead. Ducking under the overhang, he stepped inside and quickly assessed his surroundings--no unfriendly beasts and no looming threats from dark passages. It was warm and dry inside and he felt safe as he sat gazing through the rain at the trail, wondering.

It was late afternoon when the rain stopped, and he returned to his vessel to retrieve his knapsack before nightfall. He gathered wood and speared a fish from the shallow pool near the waterfall then returned to his new cave home. After his evening meal, he curled up snugly in his bedroll with visions of the Ascetic swimming in his brain.

Chapter 2

The Prophecy

Aleph slept soundly then awoke at first light to the forest's morning sounds. He gathered berries and fruits for his breakfast then followed his curiosity up the trail. Soon the winding path split in two. He chose the one to the right. It branched again, then again, and by noon he was hopelessly lost in the depths of the forest.

As he frantically searched for a familiar landmark, he was startled by the appearance of a tall, slim, dark figure, standing little more than a stone's throw away. Heart pounding, he strained to see the stranger's face but it was shaded by a hooded robe. "Who are you?" he called anxiously.

"I am the Guide," the stranger said. "Follow me." Before Aleph could ask where he was being led, the figure turned and disappeared into the forest. Aleph grabbed his knapsack and ran to catch him. The Guide maintained a brisk clip and Aleph found himself frequently scrambling to keep up the pace.

The path rose sharply through the thick forest, winding its way upward around the slope of the great mountain. As they ascended, vegetation became increasingly sparse and the air grew cool. Oak gave way to pine, then pine to scrub and scrub to rock. Emerging onto a rocky field high on the slope, the Guide stopped and pointed ahead with his staff.

Aleph crawled out onto the rocks then stood to see to where the Guide was pointing. He immediately recognized the gnarled peak of Mt. Erudite and then he spotted a wisp of smoke rising from just below the summit. As he turned to ask the Guide about it he found himself quite alone. Shrugging, he turned and set out across the rock pasture which lay before him. Soon a large cave with a small clearing at its mouth came into view. An old man was sitting quietly by the fire. Aleph's heart pounded wildly in his chest. He had found the Ascetic! His eyes grew wide with wonder and anticipation as the old man looked up from the fire and beckoned him to approach.

A chair hewn from an old tree stump sat near the fire. It was obviously placed there for guests and Aleph eased himself forward and into it. He circled his hands slowly over the fire, warming himself against the morning chill as he studied the Ascetic's face intently. Those eyes! Those penetrating blue eyes! Aleph had never seen eyes that striking shade of blue before, and they were all the more entrancing against the Ascetic's flowing white beard.

Aleph wanted to speak, but could not single out one thought from his muddled mind. He wished the Ascetic would take the lead and speak first but the old man just sat there staring at the fire, stirring it occasionally. Finally, Aleph could stand it no longer and broke the silence. "I am Aleph of Carpathia, made Outlander for following The Way."

The Ascetic looked up from the fire and fixed his eyes on Aleph's face. Aleph gripped the seat of his chair, overpowered by the Ascetic's consuming gaze. "I've been expecting you, Aleph," the Ascetic said. "Welcome!"

Aleph's head jerked up, his eyes widened, his breath quickened. "And just how is it that you know my name; and how did you know I was coming?"

"I know those who follow The Way," the Ascetic replied warmly with a kind smile.

Aleph looked intently into the old man's time-hewn face. The rosy cheeks, the curious tilt of his head, the wrinkles at the corners of his eyes, and his eyes--those tranquil cobalt pools that captured Aleph's very soul. This was a face of kindness and Aleph began to relax. "I feel that justice has been ill served to me," Aleph said. "I was banished for following The Way and consider my punishment quite excessive."

"If you choose to indulge yourself in what is just or unjust, you should follow The Precepts," the Ascetic said. "The Way is for those who do not want what they deserve. The Way is for those who seek mercy."

"I followed The Way to find the comfort I was seeking, Tbut it has only brought me loneliness," Aleph said, "and loneliness is a poor companion."

"Then why not live your life like the Hedons--immerse yourself in revelry to avoid the loneliness?" the Ascetic asked.

8

"I have seen the eyes of those who abandon themselves to purposeless merriment and I judge their loneliness even greater than mine. They are ghosts with blank stares of breathing death." Aleph shook his head. "No, Ascetic, I do not wish to spend my life seizing and squeezing every breath of decadence from my remaining time."

"Perhaps you will be one who never grows comfortable with your beliefs."

"And if I do not, what will happen to me?" Aleph asked.

"You will continue to find challenges," the Ascetic replied. "You will continue to grow. You will not join the ranks of the chosen frozen!"

"I only want to do what is right."

"And where do you suppose you will get the wisdom to judge what is right?" the Ascetic asked.

"What do you mean?" Aleph asked. "I have been taught right from wrong all my life."

"When things turn out the way you believe they should, you label them right. When things do not turn the way you believe they should, you label them wrong. Unfortunately, you cannot draw logical conclusions from emotional experiences. It is better for now that you look only to the consequences of your actions and judge them by your pain, for what is right for one may not be right for another."

Aleph gazed longingly out to sea. "I spent much time thinking about my consequences for following The Way while I drifted out there," he said. "My consequences were grave, but I cannot believe that following The Way is wrong for me." He was quiet for a time. "Why is The Way so misunderstood?" he finally asked.

The Ascetic smiled. "Perhaps it is not misunderstood. Perhaps it is only feared as something which might lead people away from the church."

"Ah, the church!" Aleph exclaimed. "The only thing which has caused me more pain than following The Way. It angers me to see the Churchwardens hawking salvation to those who fear punishment. They multiply their coffers in proportion to the amount of terror they can instill in their followers."

"Are there not those of the church who do right?" asked the Ascetic.

"Well," Aleph said thoughtfully, "many do perform good deeds, but they do so only for selfish reasons. They believe that if they are good enough and perform the right ceremonies they can earn their way into the Place of Eternal Comfort."

"Then which is the greater sin, Aleph, doing wrong for the right reason or doing right for the wrong reason?"

"Is it not The Way to give and to serve without thought of reward?" Aleph asked.

"That is The Way," the Ascetic replied. "And if you believe it, you will not need the reward of knowing what good you have done."

"But I sometimes think that my very existence depends upon having a purpose for my existence," Aleph said. "When I have no purpose, I have no hope, no future. If I can have no hope and no future, then I welcome death. I have seen many a life taken by its own hand when all noble reasons for living were lost."

"Then would your death serve a greater purpose than your life?" the old man asked.

"I am not wise enough to judge such things, right?" Aleph replied sarcastically. "Ascetic, how am I ever to know my direction?"

The Ascetic smiled. "Some follow because they do not know how to lead. Others lead because they do not know how to follow. It matters not what direction you choose, for even if you think it wrong, you will learn something."

Aleph gazed into the fire. "You are certainly right about one thing--I do not have the wisdom to judge right from wrong."

"Then how do you know I am right?" the Ascetic asked with a smile.

Aleph chuckled. "Point well taken," he said, then his face grew somber. "The Churchwardens claim that you are evil. They do everything in their power to discredit your teachings."

"And just what is it that they do to my discredit?" the Ascetic asked.

"They point to your Prophecy of the Lost to frighten those who do not understand The Way. When people are taught that *those who follow The Way shall be lost to the world*, they cling ever tighter to the Precepts which they understand and shun The Way which they do not."

The Ascetic shook his head. "Church leaders write doctrine and governments pass laws because they are afraid that their followers will be lost, and in so doing they cause people to be lost. Fear is always a self-fulfilling prophecy."

"Was it from the Prophecy of the Lost that their fear came?"

"It was from their fear that the Prophecy of the Lost came," replied the Ascetic.

"But I am like them," Aleph said. "I am afraid of being lost."

"It is not being lost that you fear," replied the Ascetic. "You already *are* lost. It is those who are not lost who fear being lost."

"Then have I fallen victim to that Prophecy?" Aleph asked.

"You have fulfilled the Prophecy," the Ascetic replied. "It is because you are lost that you have been chosen from many for a great and noble purpose."

"And just what is that purpose?" Aleph asked, wrinkling his brow.

"It is for you, Aleph, to fulfill a new Prophecy." Their eyes met, and the Ascetic's cool gaze captured Aleph's very soul. "From the House of Aleph shall descend the Keeper of the Trees, and a haven for the lost shall welcome him."

Aleph's pulse quickened as he sensed that something of great import was being told to him. "And just who or what is the Keeper of the Trees?" he asked inquisitively.

The Ascetic smiled warmly and leaned forward, capturing Aleph with his eyes. "He is one who shall bring The Way of freedom to the world," he replied. "He shall come with the passing of the Star and his passing shall be with the coming of the Star."

Aleph's eyes widened, his jaw dropped, his shoulders drew back as he sat up straight in his chair. "Why would someone such as this seek welcome in a haven for the lost?" he asked.

"He will not be of this world," the Ascetic replied. "He will be lost in it."

Aleph stared in awe, confused and confounded. "Very well then," he said, "but what are the Trees?"

"Alas," the Ascetic said, "you shall never know them, but they shall be used to build a bridge across the Valley of Eternity, joining death to life that all may cross. They shall offer The Way for regrets to give way to gratitude, sorrow to joy, anger to forgiveness, selfishness to love, pride to humility, and fear to faith."

Aleph was silent for a moment, trying to assimilate what the Ascetic had told him. "And what is my part?" he finally asked with cautious skepticism.

"The House of Aleph shall direct a light that the Outlanders of the world might discover The Way home from darkness. You shall create a sanctuary,

11

a haven for the misunderstood, that the lost might find the lost, for those who are not lost are not seeking them. The lost are the chosen ones, you know."

Aleph laid his chin in his hand and thought for a moment. "If being lost is such a noble state," he finally said, "then why does it cause so much pain, so much sorrow?"

"It is only those in darkness who yearn for light," the Ascetic replied, "and in their seeking and yearning their souls are nourished."

"Being lost in darkness is certainly reason enough to seek something," Aleph said.

"Have you not heard that it is toward those in the deepest darkness that The Life That Is directs its brightest beacon? Light only has purpose when there is darkness to illuminate."

Aleph shook his head. "Perhaps what you are telling me will make sense some day, but for now I am happy just knowing that my life does have purpose, even if I do not fully understand what it is."

"When you are not sure what your purpose is to be, your purpose is to be," the Ascetic said. "Trust the urge of The Life That Is and the purpose of your being will be revealed."

Suddenly Aleph hunched his shoulders, hung his head and began to cry.

"What is it, Aleph?" the Ascetic asked.

Aleph rubbed his eyes on the sleeve of his robe. "It's just that I doubt my faith. Perhaps I have been blinded by my experience with the Churchwardens and their sanctified hypocrisy."

"When you allow hypocrites to stand between you and The Life That Is, perhaps you would do well to notice who is standing closer."

"But their beliefs and actions often defy logic, and I place great faith in logic," Aleph said.

"Faith is not always logical nor does logic always prove faithful," replied the Ascetic. "You have tried to make faith a product of logic, but logic is a product of faith. It is only people of faith who have a logical idea of what life is all about."

"Then how does one discover faith?" Aleph asked.

"It is The Way to give what you know of yourself to what you know of The Life That Is," the Ascetic replied. "Each time you do, more of both will be shown to you."

Aleph sat frozen to his spot, back straight, hands gripping the arms of the chair. With all the sincerity he could muster, he squared his shoulders and leaned forward. "Some of your words confuse and confound me, Ascetic, but whatever it is I am to do, I am willing."

"What I have told you will have meaning some day," the Ascetic said.

Though Aleph did not fully understand, an enormous sense of responsibility welled up from deep within him. Suddenly, his life held new possibility and he wanted so very much to face his duty bravely. He had a hundred questions but long shadows laced their surroundings and the Ascetic brought their visit to a close. "Your journey is long and night approaches. The Guide will lead you back down the path."

"Will I see you again?" Aleph asked.

"Take this crystal and wear it around your neck," the Ascetic said as he handed Aleph a pendant.

Aleph took the crystal which dangled from a thin strip of deer hide. It was clear and sparkling, and its facets caught the light, turning it into every color of the rainbow. Aleph was awed by its dazzling brilliance as he held it and stared.

"When you wish to call the Guide," the Ascetic continued, "raise it high in the sunlight. The Guide will come."

The Ascetic had no sooner finished speaking than the Guide appeared at Aleph's shoulder. Aleph rose reluctantly and followed his lead. As they started back down toward the rocky meadow, Aleph turned for one last glimpse of the Ascetic, and waved a final farewell.

It was near midnight when they returned to the western slope of the great mountain and to the spot where they had first met. The Guide pointed to the path which would take Aleph back to his cave and then vanished into the darkness of the forest.

Back in the safety of his cave and the warmth of his bedroll, Aleph recounted his visit. Suddenly, he was aware of the magnitude of his responsibility, and he heaved a long sigh as the Ascetic's words played over and over in his mind--*from the House of Aleph shall descend the Keeper of the Trees, and a haven for the lost shall welcome him.*

Chapter 3

The Meeting

Days passed, then weeks, and Aleph ventured further into the interior hoping to find a village, a camp, another human, but in vain. Realizing that he was quite alone in his paradise, save for the Guide and the Ascetic, he settled into the task of making a life for himself.

His new-found world was a generous one indeed. The forest was filled with fruits and berries, the streams were teeming with fish and there was wildlife in abundance.

It was early spring. Aleph was tracking a deer that he hoped would provide meat for some weeks to come. As he crept quietly along the bank of a stream his hunt was sharply interrupted. There, right before his disbelieving eyes, was a young woman, about his age, bathing and washing her robes in the middle of the stream. She was small, delicate, almost fragile, but her fair naked skin and jet black hair made her a striking creature indeed.

She was quite oblivious to his presence as he watched her movements and listened to her beautiful voice humming unfamiliar songs. When she had finished bathing, she pulled her clothing on over her head and waded up to the bank. Her thin white robes fell about her in tatters, though he could see that they were once fine garments. She seated herself on a rock by the stream and began brushing her hair with a crude, makeshift brush.

For more than an hour, he watched her intently and the longer he watched and listened, the more he longed for her companionship. Finally, he decided to make his presence known, though he did not wish to frighten her away. "Hello there!" he called from a distance. "My name is Aleph."

14

With one smooth, swift motion, she swung toward him, picked up a rock, planted her feet squarely apart, hunched forward and drew her arm back. She was poised to fight or to run at the first sign of danger.

Aleph was taken aback by the ferocity of her stance. She may have been petite of body, but there was nothing timid about her spirit. "You have no reason to fear me," he called, still keeping his distance. "I wish you no harm."

She relaxed her stance, lowered the rock to her side and stood upright, though she still stared at him through cautious eyes.

"I live on the south side of the island," he continued, "where the great mountain meets the sea. I thought myself alone until now." He paused for a reply, but none came. "Do you understand me?"

She slowly nodded affirmatively and Aleph continued. "Since we share this land, I would like to know more about you and I shall tell you everything about me."

She remained silent, still suspicious.

"Very well," he said, "I sense your fear and shall not impose myself upon you. Rather, I shall invite you to come to know me as your trust permits. I shall camp there, in the clearing near the river in plain sight so you can see my movements."

She glanced to where he was pointing, then back to him and slowly nodded again. He did not see her for the rest of the day, and by nightfall he assumed she had fled. Sleep came slowly as he lay there thinking of her and he awoke early with her still on her mind.

The sun was just beginning to peek over the horizon when he stumbled from his bed roll and ambled groggily toward the stream, sat on his haunches and began to splash cold water on his face. Just then he caught a glimpse of her out of the corner of his eye. She was watching him cautiously from the bushes.

He began spearing fish for breakfast, pretending he had not seen her. After he had caught several, he decided to try talking with her once more. "The stream has been generous today," he called without turning. "My creel is full, and I would be honored if you would share my catch."

Silence still. He shrugged and returned to his camp. He built a fire and sharpened sticks to skewer his catch for cooking. With the fish broiling slowly over the fire, he sat relaxing on a nearby log and sipped a cup of herb tea he had brewed. Looking in her direction, he could see her creeping closer, and by the time the fish were done, she had come all the way into his camp and seated herself on a log, keeping the fire between them. She remained guarded, watching his every movement for any sign of threat, but apparently willing to connect.

"I am Aleph, outcast from Carpathia," Aleph said as took a skewered fish from the fire and held it out toward her.

"And I am Anna, outcast from Malthus," she said as she took the fish and laid it on a Catalpa leaf to cool.

"I have been here for a year now," Aleph said. "How long since you came?"

"Only three moons," Anna replied. "What was your crime?"

"I followed The Way of The Ascetic. Do you know of The Way?"

"Yes, it is forbidden in our land as well, but I, too, have followed it," she replied. "Do you believe that the Ascetic is real?"

"I do," Aleph replied.

"Do you believe that he is a prophet of The Life That Is?" she asked.

"A few even claim that he *is* The Life That Is, manifest in the flesh," Aleph replied. "The legends tell of his honesty of word, generosity of cup and kindness to all living things."

"The legends also say that he lives here in Oxymora, but I have seen no sign of *anyone* until you came along," she said.

Aleph said nothing. He was afraid Anna would think him mad if he told her he had been to visit this legendary being.

"How did you become interested in The Way?" Anna asked.

"I am not sure whether it was my curiosity about the legends or my admiration for the Waysayers," Aleph replied. "I only know that I was afraid all the time and the Waysayers were the only ones who did not allow fear to rule them. Even during the Year of the Star, they remained calm amid the chaos. They gave me hope that I could be rid of my fear."

"It is often difficult to have hope in the face of the Star," Anna said. "It is understandable that you would want to be like them."

"I did not care if I were like them, but I wanted to know how to control my fear like they did," Aleph replied. "Fear has been my enemy since I can remember and they had learned to conquer it, but they also offered so much more. They offered enlightenment as an alternative to the safety of tradition."

"And did you join them?" she asked.

"I was eighteen when they took me into their ranks. That was three years ago and my life has been in chaos ever since. I did not yet understand discretion and, in my excitement, I spoke my truth openly. When I did, I learned the hard way that defying the Churchwardens is no way to endear yourself to them. They took their time, built their case and made sure I would never return." Aleph was beginning to choke back tears. "And just what sinister crime did you commit?" he asked, wishing to avoid reliving his banishment.

She hunched toward the fire and hugged herself. "After I started following The Way, I spoke out against my father," she replied, tears welling in her eyes.

"That hardly seems a crime deserving of banishment. If all children who spoke out against their parents were banished, whole generations would be floating at sea."

"My father is Vistar, Monarch of Malthus," she continued. "My family is among the wealthiest of Malthusian aristocracy. Our wealth came from the flint. . . ."

"Of course!" Aleph interrupted. "Malthusian flint is highly prized. It is much sought after in Carpathia."

"It is the only thing that keeps Malthus alive," she said. "There are a few fertile fields and sparse forests, but only along the river valleys. Most of our landscape is dominated by rocky ground that is unyielding of even the most meager crops. The flint has been our salvation. My father is the one who developed our flint trade, but he is also the one who controls it. The people who purchase our flint pay exorbitant prices out of their need, our workers receive peasant wages for their toil, and my father increases his profits. My board and bed grew less and less hospitable with knowledge of how it was purchased."

"And so you spoke your truth much as I did," Aleph said as the picture became a little more clear.

Anna nodded. "I said enough to bring my father under scrutiny by Carpathian diplomats and to cause a great deal of unrest among our workers. The only way he could save face was to discredit me."

Aleph shook his head. "But you had so much to lose!" he said. "I *had* no parents. I *had* no home. I had nothing. But you, in your station--why would you jeopardize such a thing?"

17

The Keeper of the Trees

"Come now Aleph," she said, "if you truly follow The Way you know that riches and power and recognition provide no kind of security and they certainly do not keep one noble or make one happy."

"Yes, I do know that," Aleph replied sheepishly. "It's just that I have never lived in luxury. I would not know what it is like to have such comforts. It must have been very painful for you."

"To witness the gods of wealth and power demand my sacrifice was almost more than I could bear," Anna replied. "I was numb with disbelief when my father stood before the court and read charges of sedition against me. I was nothing more than another casualty in his war against his own vulnerability."

"But how did you find your way here? How did you find Oxymora?"

"It was not by my own hand that I was guided, for I set no course," Anna said. "For days I drifted upon the tide, yielding my fate to the prevailing winds, finding reason to neither live nor die, not really caring which would choose me. But when I saw the high rock cliffs appear on the horizon, I suddenly longed for land. I set my course southward, and spent the next three days weaving my way between the sharp jags of the great stone reef, barely missing them at times. I was exhausted from the endless motion of the sea but could find no harbor."

"The reef has been explored many times by many men," Aleph said, "but no one ever found a harbor, and many were dashed upon the rocks for their efforts. That is why seafarers abandoned their explorations of Oxymora long ago. Where did you come ashore?"

"I became trapped in a narrow passage between the cliffs," Anna replied. "Just when I thought I would surely be smashed by the next wave, my vessel was swept into an inlet which is walled off from the sea by the reef. I navigated through the inlet and a different world emerged. The waters grew calm, a broad sandy beach framed by rock ledges stretched before me, a meandering stream gently spilled itself into the harbor and lush greenery lay beyond. I followed the river valley inland and found a garden of plenty."

"It sounds a lot like the cove I found. Just where is this harbor?"

"It lies across the valley beyond the bend in the river," she said. "A branch of this river spills into it."

"I should like to see it," Aleph said.

"Very well," she said. "I do not think you intend me any harm. I shall take you there." They gathered their things and set out for Anna's Cove. As they strolled along the river bank, they shared more about themselves with one another.

It was dusk when they reached Anna's Cove and they were both very tired. They placed their bed rolls together and lay beside one another, and before the night had ended, they were entwined. Each was lonely for companionship and they provided warmth and comfort for one another, something neither had experienced in far too long.

Aleph awoke as the sun was beginning to fill the cove with a new day. Anna had been awake for some time. She had built a fire and was brewing tea of roots she had foraged. Aleph got up and moved toward the fire. He sat and huddled himself into a ball, pulling his blanket around his shoulders. She handed him a cup of warm tea and sat beside him, and they stayed there for a long while, each a little less lonely.

Chapter 4

Setting Boundaries

Under different circumstances it is not likely that Aleph and Anna would have been attracted to one another, but both preferred the security, safety and companionship that togetherness provided, and each compromised a little to make their union more bearable.

Over the next few weeks, they explored their new land together. Heading north, they discovered massive forests, clean and untouched. To the east and west, mountain ranges and slopes rose and fell with undulating grace, forming the rim of a great bowl, punctuated by Mount Erudite to the south. The heart of the land cradled fertile valleys with winding streams crisscrossing in playful patterns.

Their explorations eventually brought them full circle back to Aleph's Cave. It was a near-perfect location and their surroundings provided for all their needs. The Dark Forest which bordered on the north and east provided medicines, food, and building materials, the Paradise Valley which lay to the west yielded fish and game in abundance, and Aleph's Landing to the south offered welcome harbor to anyone who might venture their way. And so, together, Aleph and Anna settled into daily living in the shadow of Mount Erudite. The rich land embraced and enfolded them and they continued their lives in peaceful isolation.

The cave provided adequate sleeping quarters, but they both desired more space with increased comforts and, room by room, they built a circular structure with rock walls and a thatched roof covered with Catalpa leaves. One room was for fire-building and cooking, another for making garments, tools and implements, and yet another for just sitting and relaxing, but Anna's favorite room was the bath. A continuous stream of cool, clear water diverted from a nearby waterfall provided a luxurious fountain where Anna could bathe and wash clothing without having to journey to the stream. In the center of this circular fortress stood a lush open garden accessible from each of the surrounding rooms, and an atrium connected this inner garden to a covered veranda which overlooked the ocean to the south. It was their home, and they called it Bonaventure.

By the time a year had passed, they had settled into a comfortable rhythm with one another, and day-by-day a fondness grew between them as each found new respect for the other. That is not to say that life together was not without its problems--Anna had become increasingly moody lately, and her irritability reached a peak one spring day while she was fidgeting over their lunch.

"Anna, you seem restless today. Are you upset about something?" Aleph asked.

"It is nothing that you can fix," she replied despondently.

"But if something is wrong, I must know about it."

"Very well, Aleph, sometimes I just feel a little smothered."

"Then let us take a trip," Aleph suggested. Perhaps you need a change of scenery. We could go north and see. . . ."

"No, Aleph!" Anna interrupted. "There are just some things you cannot make better. It is not the place that is the problem."

"Then what is it?" he insisted.

"I'm not sure I know," Anna replied. "I just feel trapped sometimes. Perhaps I miss my independence. I have not been apart from you since the day we met, and sometimes I just want my own life."

"But your life is with me, now. I need you."

"You do not need me nearly so much as you need for me to need you, Aleph," Anna said. "Sometimes I just need to need myself."

"But it is my duty to protect you and keep you from harm, and it is a duty that I relish."

"That is exactly what I mean, Aleph. It is *my* duty to protect me and keep me from harm. I do not seek your protection and I often resent your implication that I need it. It is an imposition upon my rights and my freedom."

"But Anna. . . ." Aleph's protest was interrupted as Anna ran out the door and toward the stream.

The Keeper of the Trees

Aleph could see that he was getting nowhere with this, and decided to leave well enough alone. He had learned to keep his distance from her discontent.

Except for Anna's occasional outbursts, all was essentially well--all, that is, except for one glaring omission on Aleph's part--he had not yet told Anna of meeting the Ascetic. She knew nothing of the Prophecy or of her potential role in it. Aleph chose his time carefully and one fall morning while Anna was washing clothes at the river, he approached her from the bank and called to her. "Anna, we must talk."

Anna put down the clothing and sat herself on a rock, giving Aleph her full attention. "What is it, Aleph? What's troubling you?"

Aleph sat on the bank, hugged his knees to his chest and continued. "There is something I have not told you that you have a right to know."

Anna smiled and cocked her head inquisitively.

"The Ascetic is real," he suddenly blurted out. "I have seen him, talked with him, and he has given me a prophecy."

"Well, what a marvelous thing!" Anna said a bit sarcastically as she straightened her back and folded her arms. "Such a small thing! And just why did you feel the need to keep it a secret for so long?"

"I suppose I thought you would not believe me, or that you would think me mad, or that you would not wish to become mixed up with it."

Aleph waited for a reaction from her, but she just sat there, back straight, legs crossed, arms folded, expressionless. He continued. "The Ascetic told me that I am to father a sanctuary, a haven for the lost. Oxymora is to become a haven for the Outlanders of the world."

"I see," said Anna. "And is there more?"

"Yes, there is more," Aleph replied. "The Prophecy also says that from the House of Aleph shall descend a chosen one who shall be known as the Keeper of the Trees."

Anna glared at Aleph, visibly angry now. "And I suppose that this is the part that involves me!" she said.

"Anna, I have been slow to promise, for it is said that promises carefully made are those most often fulfilled. I have thought it through carefully and I wish to offer you my promise."

22

Anna stood up in the stream, legs firmly apart, hands on her hips, lips pursed, eyes squinted. "And you think that your promise would be worth something to me after living with your falsehood?"

"Anna, why are you angry with me? I did not lie to you. I simply did not tell you everything."

"A truth omitted is no better than a lie told," Anna replied.

"I understand how you feel, Anna, but what about my promise?"

"Do you not see that when you place so much value on promises, you discount the living we have done since the beginning? I do not need your promise! If there has been no commitment until now, then what possible value could your promise hold, especially since you know so little of your future?"

"I'm sorry, Anna, I just. . . ."

"I have always considered your aspirations noble, Aleph," she interrupted, "and I committed myself to you the night we first lay together. I have been committed from the very beginning to share your life, be your mate, and bear your children. It was meant to be or it would not be."

"I don't know what to say, Anna. I never knew you felt that way," Aleph said as he stretched out his hand and helped her up to the bank. As they sat there together, side by side, Aleph put his arm around her, and from that moment forward, *promise* was never mentioned again.

Telling Anna his secret freed Aleph of worrying over it, and Anna did not hold her anger for long. It was spring of their third year and, all in all, life was good. Aleph had not concerned himself with the Prophecy for some time, but his life of peaceful complacency was not to last. Aleph began to ponder the Prophecy. By summer, his pondering had turned to worry and by fall, the Ascetic's words ran incessantly through his mind. He dreaded the setting of the sun, for it was at night more than any other time that his ruminations consumed him. Night after night, his frustration rose as his challenge to father a haven for Outlanders was being met with helplessness, impotence. He frequently took the piece of crystal from around his neck and held it tightly in his fist as he lay in his bed, wondering if he should summon the Guide.

On one such restless night as Aleph tossed fretfully, his frustration reached a peak. Thinking he might go mad, he arose and left the cave.

Anna watched quietly as he stood in the moonlight shaking his head and wringing his hands, and soon she joined him to try to comfort him. "What is it, Aleph?" she asked, as she approached him from behind and placed her hand gently on his shoulder.

"It is the Prophecy, Anna. What if I fail to live up to my part in the Prophecy?"

"What is it you think you should be doing?" Anna asked.

"I don't know exactly. I only know that time is passing me by and nothing of the Prophecy has come to pass."

"Must you always have something to worry over, Aleph? Your obsessions are often difficult to understand and even more difficult to tolerate."

"Why are you so upset with me, Anna?"

"I don't know," Anna replied. "Perhaps it's just that I spend so much time trying to appease your ego. You have obsessed over my happiness since the day we met, yet it is not in your power to make me happy, and the harder you try, the more miserable I become."

"I know that we have argued, but did not know that you were so unhappy," Aleph said, hanging his head.

"It is sometimes difficult to live with someone who sees himself as controller of the world," Ann snapped.

"What do you mean, Anna?"

"I mean that you cannot force the Prophecy to come true any more than you can force me to be happy. Sometimes the more force you apply, the more resistance you meet. Do you not believe that all these things will happen in due time?"

"I'm not sure what to believe anymore, Anna. The Prophecy foretold of a haven for the lost, and yet there are no lost seeking haven here. The Prophecy foretold that the Keeper of the Trees shall descend from the House of Aleph, and yet we have no children. What if I have already failed?"

Anna shook her head. "Perhaps it is not up to you to cause failure or success to happen. Perhaps it is in the hands of fate."

"You sound like the Ascetic," Aleph said.

"Why don't you summon the Guide with the crystal and visit the Ascetic?" Anna asked. "The Ascetic will surely advise you."

"Perhaps I should," Aleph replied. "Perhaps I should."

With that, Anna returned to her bed, leaving him there the remainder of the night. When the sun broke over the horizon, Aleph closed his eyes, took the crystal from around his neck, and held it toward the sky with both hands. He was a little amazed and a lot relieved when the Guide appeared and touched him on the shoulder. The crystal worked!

Aleph scrambled to his feet and, without a word, followed the Guide toward the trail. There was a spring in Aleph's step as he chased the Guide briskly up the mountain. As they climbed, the sun moved slowly up in the sky and by noon they were in the presence of the Ascetic.

Aleph sat himself once more in the stump chair and relaxed for the first time in a long while. The Ascetic's camp was a safe and cozy place indeed, with the mountain cave providing an impenetrable backdrop to the brush-fenced clearing. As he sat there by the fire, he basked in its golden glow and marveled at the radiance it reflected on the Ascetic's face. He felt warm and comforted, at peace and at ease.

The Ascetic handed him some warm tea and Aleph began to unravel his tangled thoughts. "I no longer dwell alone," he began. "I have found a mate and her name is Anna. Together, we have explored this land from the forests in the north, to the cove in the west, to the great mountain range in the east. We have made a home at the base of this mountain and there we dwell as one."

"And are you happy?" asked the Ascetic.

"Well, our chores are halved and our comforts doubled," Aleph replied. "We are each a little less lost now that we have found one other." He paused for a reply but none came. "But things are not always good between us," he continued, hanging his head. "Our disagreements are many and our differences are resolved only with great effort. Ascetic, I know that I must join with someone if the Prophecy is to be fulfilled, and it seems all too obvious that Anna is to be the one, though I have not given her my promise. I tried to once, but it angered her greatly."

"It is not what you promise that matters," the Ascetic said. "The only real commitment lies in the doing. Commitment is about promising little and doing much."

"But I fear that without promise, she will not be bound to stay with me."

"Promises given out of fear of loss often cause the loss you fear," the Ascetic said. "If your need for security outweighs your love, you will struggle with each thing you desire until it becomes exhausted."

"But if we do not exchange our promise. . . ."

"Exchange?" the Ascetic interrupted with eyebrows raised. "Then you also expect a promise in return?"

"Of course!" Aleph replied. If there is not promise in return, then how will I know if there is love?"

"Love cannot be proved by promise," the Ascetic replied, "and demanding its proof often kills the love that is there. If it is love, it expects nothing--not promise, not fulfillment, not happiness, not even love returned."

Aleph hung his head. "Then I fear that choosing love may require more than I can give."

"It matters not what you choose, for if it is love, it shall choose you," the Ascetic said. The Ascetic then peered into the old black kettle which simmered on the edge of the fire. "Look into this caldron and tell me what you see."

Aleph looked up into the Ascetic's eyes, stood slowly and peeked tentatively over the edge of the large, steamy pot. "I see my reflection," he said, looking back at the Ascetic. "Just what should I see?"

"There is much that lies beneath the surface," replied the Ascetic. "Your surface shines with selfishness, but it reflects the fear which lies beneath."

"What does my fear have to do with selfishness?" Aleph asked.

"It is fear that causes selfishness and selfishness that causes fear," replied the Ascetic.

Aleph returned his gaze to the kettle and looked himself in the eye once more. "It is not hard to admit that I am selfish, Ascetic. Were it up to me, I would choose a mate who would coddle me, agree with me, and do my bidding rather than one who aggravates and argues."

"Do you know what it is that you fear, Aleph?" the Ascetic asked.

Aleph thought for a moment. "I suppose I fear abandonment," he said, hanging his head again.

"And your fear of abandonment causes you to seek a guarantee about your future?" the Ascetic asked.

"So it would seem," Aleph admitted, looking back into the Ascetic's eyes.

"Aleph, have you not looked to others to fill the emptiness in you before?" the Ascetic asked.

"I have," Aleph replied reluctantly.

"And when it did not get filled, did you not blame them for your loneliness?"

"I did," Aleph admitted.

"Then do you suppose it wise to look to Anna to fill your emptiness now?"

Aleph was quiet for a time, staring out to sea. "I suppose I must look to myself," he finally replied.

"It is only when you are completely filled that you will have enough left over for another. Become perfectly at one in your aloneness and you will become perfectly at one in your togetherness."

"But what of the flaws in each of us?" Aleph asked.

"Everything that is of The Life That Is has flaws. If love waited for flawless creatures there would be only waiting."

Aleph nodded and sat thoughtfully for a time. "Perhaps the reason people follow the Precepts is that they are so much easier to understand than The Way," he said. "The Precepts say that if you love someone, you love them *in spite of* their flaws. You overlook their defect, ignore their imperfections."

The Ascetic looked into Aleph's face and smiled. "If you love *in spite of* flaws, it means you do not love the whole person. It means you love the best and ignore the rest. The Way says that love *embraces* flaws, for flaws are as much a part of the whole as that which is whole."

Aleph nodded once more, then was silent for a time before he spoke. "You have given me many new thoughts, Ascetic," he finally said, "and I shall do my utmost to take them into my heart. Perhaps then Anna and I can not only *dwell* as one, we can truly *be* as one."

"To be as two lightens the burden," the old man said, smiling as the Guide approached them. "And now I must bid you goodby."

When Aleph returned, he found Anna sitting on the Promontory Point. She was huddled forward, arms hugging her knees to her chest, chin resting on her arm. He approached her slowly, not wishing to disturb her thoughts.

"You are back," she said without turning. "Did the Ascetic give you guidance?"

"He showed me that I must let what is, be," Aleph said softly.

Anna turned, took his hand in hers and looked into his eyes. "I hope you have not misunderstood me, Aleph," she said, "I believe in the Prophecy and I believe in you."

Tears filled Aleph's eyes as he fell to his knees and into her arms, sobbing. Anna held his head to her breast. "I want you to know that I want your children, and I want to help make this a place of welcome for outcasts. Together, we shall do all we can to contribute our part to the fulfillment of the Ascetic's foretelling."

Aleph held her tightly and continued to sob. It was all the promise he needed.

Chapter 5

Found at Last

For the next seven years, Aleph and Anna remained faithful to their purpose. With the coming of each new season, they carved messages of welcome into dried birch wood and set their hopes adrift. Their invitation was a simple one: *If you are lost, you are welcome. Aleph and Anna of Oxymora.*

Each morning, they descended the well-worn path to the Promontory Point and searched the seas to the west, the south and the east, hoping against hope to set sight on tall sails piercing the horizon. Seven years and no sign that their invitation had been received by anyone, and yet they maintained their vigil.

It was a crisp morning in early fall when Aleph spied the small dot on the distant horizon to the south. Filled with excitement, he and Anna scurried down to Aleph's Landing and lit a signal fire. Their persistence had finally paid off, their steadfastness had been rewarded. The ship was sailing directly toward their island home and the ship's crew responded by hoisting their flag of peace.

As the ship approached the bay, Aleph could see that it was one of the few magnificent vessels built in his homeland of Carpathia. Its beautiful mahogany hull could carry sufficient goods and produce to supply a city of three hundred people for a year. Its quarters could house twenty men. Its three masts which flew seven sails could speed it to every land in the known world four times a year.

Suddenly, Aleph raised his brow and a broad grin spread across his face. "Look, Anna! It is *The Adventurer*."

Anna stared blankly into Aleph's face. "It is obvious that you know of this vessel, but it is not familiar to me," she said.

"Surely you have heard of *The Adventurer* and of Oberon, the famous merchant seaman who trades between Carpathia and Malthus," Aleph replied.

"Oh, of course!" replied Anna, "I remember hearing tales of Oberon's adventures when I was a child, and he was in my father's house once when I was very young. I remember sitting on his lap and looking up into his flaming red beard. His face was all weathered from too many days at sea, but his eyes sparkled and his nose and cheeks were always rosy. He nearly tossed me off his lap with his boisterous laugh."

"He is welcome everywhere, but claims no land as home."

They watched the ship deftly make its way into the small bay, and by mid-afternoon, *The Adventurer* was moored safely in Aleph's Cove. Oberon and two of his crew launched a dinghy toward the sandy beach where Aleph and Anna anxiously awaited.

As this small craft rounded the edge of the jagged cliffs, Anna let out a squeal. "Judith!" she shouted as she ran toward the approaching vessel. "Is it really you? I dare say that I never expected to lay eyes on your blonde locks and blue eyes again." Turning to Aleph, she explained breathlessly, "It is my oldest and dearest friend from Malthus. I cannot believe that she is really here!"

"Anna!" Judith shouted in reply. "It is a joy to see you alive!"

Oberon, grinning broadly at the recognition the two ladies exchanged, announced his greeting. " Hail, Wayfarers!" he shouted as the dinghy approached the shore. It was a familiar old greeting which spoke of friendship and good will and it warmed Aleph and Anna to hear it spoken once again.

"Hail, Wayfarers!" Aleph replied, returning the open greeting. "Welcome to Oxymora."

The bow of the dinghy slid smoothly onto the white sandy beach. "We were passing to the south enroute from Malthus to Carpathia when we fished your driftwood from the sea. Seeing that it was recently carved, we decided to venture to your shore to see who might be foolhardy enough to live in this desolate place."

"We have not seen another living soul for the past ten years, and you are a welcome sight indeed," Aleph declared.

As soon as Judith disembarked, Anna embraced her and they quickly became lost in conversation as they strolled down the beach arm in arm.

"Judith there is my scullery maid," said Oberon, "and this is her husband, Rowland, my navigator, without whom I would be eternally lost; or so he would have me believe."

They all chuckled as Rowland extended his massive hand. He was big, solid, and athletic, quite a contrast to Judith's slight, almost fragile frame.

"Welcome, Rowland," replied Aleph, taking Rowland's hand in greeting. "Welcome, welcome to all. We would be honored if you would share our table."

Aleph led their guests up the trail, and Anna and Judith soon joined them. As they sat down to a great feast, Aleph continued. "We both know of your reputation, Onagar, for Anna hails from Malthus and I from Carpathia, and tales of your adventures on the high seas are known throughout both lands."

Oberon laughed heartily and continued gorging himself on the feast they had prepared. Having taken their fill, Oberon's curiosity could wait no longer. "Just how did you two get here?"

"We were outcasts and found our way here purely by fate."

"And how is it that the two of you exist on this worthless rock?"

Aleph and Anna looked at one another and laughed, then Aleph turned back to Oberon. "This is the richest land I have ever seen. There is more here than a thousand men could take in a thousand lifetimes."

Oberon raised his eyebrows. "People from all lands have known of this forbidden place for centuries, but none have dared or desired to set foot ashore," he said. "The cliff and the reefs have kept everyone away, including me."

"We must be the first to know of its harbors," Aleph said. "There are only two, the one you see, and a larger one to the northwest." He paused. "But more about us later. Tell us what has brought you to our land."

Oberon chuckled. "My curiosity has taken me many places. It has often brought me great folly, but it has also brought me great fortune. When we fished your driftwood from the sea and Judith saw Anna's name carved into it, she persuaded me to change my course to see if it was her outcast friend."

After lunch, Judith and Anna disappeared down the beach again, talking and giggling like a couple of school girls, while Aleph and Oberon talked for the remainder of the afternoon. Aleph told of their banishment, of he and Anna finding one another, and of the hidden resources they had discovered in their new land. Oberon brought him up to date on recent events in both Malthus and Carpathia and spun tales of his adventures.

It was dusk when Anna and Judith returned, and Anna began telling Aleph about her friend. "Aleph, you and Judith have much in common. Judith was exiled for following The Way just as you were. Oberon rescued her from the open sea. She was near death when he found her."

"He employed me as his scullery maid and gave to me a life of dignity and usefulness," said Judith smiling lovingly at Oberon. "When I told him of my separation from my beloved Rowland he sent for him upon our return to Malthus and offered him a position as his navigator so he and I could be rejoined. He certainly can be a romantic rascal, considering his reputation as a rapscallion, but he hates for anyone to know it," she teased as she pulled playfully on Oberon's beard.

Oberon laughed his hearty laugh once again as he hugged the diminutive Judith to his side.

"It is late," Aleph said. Won't you share our home and our food this evening?"

Oberon agreed, and, after signaling his ship that they would be staying the night, they dined and talked well into the night. Then, they all slumbered peacefully, exhausted from the excitement of the day.

Aleph awoke early and found Oberon standing on the veranda as dawn broke over the lush green valley. "It's not exactly what you expected, is it Oberon?"

"I know of no living soul, save ourselves, who has the remotest idea that Oxymora is so fertile, so rich," Oberon replied.

Aleph looked out toward the horizon. "It's almost as if its rock walls have protected it completely, as if saving it from the world for a higher purpose."

Oberon turned and looked Aleph in the eye. "About the legend of the Ascetic--does he really exist? Have you seen him?

"He is more than legend," Aleph replied without offering any additional information, and Oberon did not interrogate him further, though he sensed that there was much left unsaid.

"Is it your wish to stay here, Aleph?" Oberon asked. "I will be happy to give you passage to anywhere you wish."

"We have no wish to leave this land," Aleph replied. "We wish to make this a haven for the Outlanders of the world. As you can see, there are rich valleys to be farmed, timbers to be felled, streams to be fished. This land yields its fruits plentifully and can sustain many without want."

Oberon's gaze shifted to the distant rocky slopes to the west. "I have seen that greenish glow before," he said. "The southern mountains of Nod once glowed with that same hue. There is only one thing which gives rock that color--those mountains are filled with copper!"

"What is copper?" Aleph asked, admitting his ignorance.

"I thought everyone had heard of copper by now," replied Oberon with a chuckle. "I forgot that you have been isolated here for these past ten years. It is a soft metal discovered over a hundred years ago by the Nodites. That is the only place copper has ever been found--until now, that is."

"And what did the Nodites do with this copper?"

"They used it to make trinkets and amulets to adorn buildings and people. I began trading with them some twenty years ago, exchanging Malthusian flint and Carpathian goods and products for their copper, gambling that this new metal would find value in other lands."

"And did it find value?"

"Not at first, but then some five or six years ago, the Nodites discovered that melting the copper together with other metals produced a substance from which tools and weapons of greater strength and durability could be forged. Suddenly, farmers plowed and harvested with greater efficiency, hunters killed with greater ease, gatherers foraged with greater productivity, and the elite traveled with greater speed and dependability."

"And no doubt the Nodites became very rich."

"Beyond your wildest dreams!" Oberon said. "When the world learned of the superiority of Nodite products, copper became highly prized. I have done little during the past five years but transport copper and copper products between Nod, Malthus and Carpathia."

"Then will you sell our copper?"

Oberon turned, grasped Aleph by the shoulders, and looked him straight in the eye. "Aleph, you have no idea what an opportunity this is," he said. "The huge demand has all but depleted the Nodite copper. The little that remains is hard to find and difficult to mine."

Aleph paused and looked at the floor, chewing his lip. "There are more important things than riches, Oberon," he said, looking back into Oberon's face. "Can you help us spread the word to Outlanders that there is a welcome haven for them here? Will you help us to find others who are lost and to bid them welcome to this place?"

Oberon laughed and patted Aleph on the shoulder. "I shall do even more," he replied. "I shall give free passage to those who wish to come, I shall carry your copper and other goods to be sold on foreign shores, and I shall bring to you all you need."

Aleph raised his eyebrows. "But why would you want to do all this?" he asked with curious skepticism.

"It has been many years since I dared to dream of such a land--virgin, yet pregnant with promise," Oberon reflected. "The possibilities of this place spark in me an excitement that I have not felt in far too long a time."

"Then just what price does your generosity carry?" asked Aleph, "for you surely will not do these things out of kindness alone."

Oberon let go a boisterous laugh. "You are perceptive Aleph, for my motives are not so noble as I might like you to think. By giving passage to people who will make this land productive, I shall be amply rewarded with the substantial profits I shall reap as a result of their labors."

"Are you saying that you intend to use these people to further your gain and to take from our land solely for your own profit?" asked Aleph, a little put off by Oberon's intentions.

"I do not *take* from anyone or anything," replied Oberon. "All my dealings are fair. I share and others share with me."

Aleph looked askance at him, a little skeptical of Oberon's assurances.

"Don't be so naive, Aleph," Oberon chuckled. "I do what I do, not out of goodness, but out of practicality. There are two things I have learned from my many years as a sea merchant. First, anything that is not equally beneficial to all is not beneficial to any. Second, a small piece of something big is far more profitable than a big piece of something small."

Aleph considered Oberon's reply for a moment, then flashed a broad grin. "Your virtue of honesty outweighs your defect of greed, Oberon!" he said, grasping his forearms. "Take from us freely and we shall trust that all you take shall bring us profit upon your return."

They gazed intently into one another's eyes, and at that moment a bond was sealed which would last the remainder of their days.

As dawn broke on the second day, Oberon, Judith and Rowland bid Aleph and Anna farewell and returned to *The Adventurer*. Aleph and Anna climbed up to the Promontory Point to watch them embark.

"We shall return when the winter has passed," Oberon shouted from the helm as they hoisted anchor and set sail for Carpathia.

Chapter 6

Trouble in Malthus

True to his word, Oberon spread the news of the haven for Outlanders throughout, bringing hope to the lost. By early spring, he had returned with a hundred seekers ready to begin a new life.

Many of the new arrivals mined the abundant copper with crude tools. The work was hard and the rewards small, but they were free. Others became merchants, bringing wares which they traded for the copper and using the copper to purchase more wares through Oberon. Still others became transporters, builders, service providers, and Oxymora flourished.

A special bond existed between Oxymora's early inhabitants. Like all who face a common peril and find a common rescue, they felt responsible to one another. Their gratitude fostered a genuine spirit of community and Oxymora became a happy and cooperative society. All who were outcast, whether by choice or decree, were welcomed, and Oxymora quickly gained a reputation for accepting without judgment, tolerating differences, and supporting freedom of thought and word. Oxymora was a place where people could think freely and act boldly. And it was not only the outcast who came. Those who were weary of ignorance, disillusioned by injustice, and sickened by moralities which treasured tradition above wisdom also sought the freedoms this new land offered.

Anna's Cove became a hub of activity. It was a near-perfect harbor, protected from the wrath of the open ocean and large enough to accommodate *The Adventurer*. Its rock ledges framed the beach on either side making ideal natural piers from which the ship could be loaded and unloaded.

As Oberon's merchant business grew, people came in growing numbers to trade copper, tools, farm implements, weapons, spices, cloth, and other items to improve their way of life. And thus was born Oxymora's first village, the village of Trada.

Trada was Oxymora's lifeline to the world. Here were warehouses the size of Oberon's ship, a teeming marketplace where goods of every description and from every land were bought and sold, pubs and lodging and eateries where weary travelers could take their fill and find rest. And, thanks to Oberon, there were docks and ships and trade.

In time, the entire world knew of the adventuresome pair who had forged a new frontier and Oxymora soon became a catcher of adventurers, a haven for the unwanted, a womb for the misunderstood. It was a montage of rebels with diverse ideals but a common need, and they all worked and lived in harmony.

It had been only ten years since Oberon first set foot upon their shores and the Year of the Star was upon them, but here there was no panic, no confusion, no controlling fear. Here there was optimism and hope.

As fall approached, Oberon sent word to Aleph and Anna that he wished an audience with them and they journeyed to Trada to greet him. They took a room in the local inn and were waiting on the pier when *The Adventurer* docked.

"Come aboard!" Oberon shouted as he lowered the plank. "It has been a long time, my friends. Dine with me. There are things we must discuss."

As they seated themselves at Oberon's table, Aleph said, "It is always an honor to dine with you, Oberon, for it was your foresight and willingness to gamble which has made our land prosperous. We are much in your debt."

Oberon chuckled. "My rewards have been ample. Neither of us owes debt to the other. Eat, drink, and then we shall talk."

When their meal was finished, Oberon poured more wine, then sat back in his chair. "I am growing weary of my life at sea and, if the Star does not destroy us, I plan to build an estate here in Trada."

Aleph almost choked on his wine. "You! On land!" he sputtered. "Your life, your home has been upon the sea."

Oberon chuckled. "I have no intentions of giving up the sea entirely," he said, "I only wish to have a place to call home."

"But why did you summon us?" Anna asked. "You know that you are welcome here."

Oberon's face grew solemn. "There is trouble in Malthus--trouble which may affect Oxymora's welfare. Your copper is rendering their flint obsolete and their flint is all they have."

"I see," replied Aleph. "And so we have become a threat to their prosperity. What do you suppose they will do?"

"If they find no remedy, they will do what any cornered animal will do--they will fight. When their own resources no longer meet their needs, they will use their might to take from others."

"Do you mean they might attack Oxymora?" Aleph asked in disbelief. "They never made war against the Nodites, why would they invade us?"

"They knew that Nodite copper was limited. The few things the Nodites did produce offered substantial competition for Malthusian flint products, but they knew it wouldn't last. But now the supply of copper is virtually limitless and the copper you sell to the Nodites ends up as tools and weapons which are superior to the flint."

"Can we not just sell our copper to Malthus?" Anna asked.

"Malthus does not have the technology to melt the copper with other metals to make it useful," Oberon replied. "What's more, they do not have the other metals."

"And the Nodites do," Anna added.

"There has been talk among the high ranks that a military take over of Oxymora is being considered," Oberon said.

"We have no desire to engage in war," Aleph said. "We have been at war with someone or something all our lives and relish the peace we have found here."

"All the more reason that you are ripe for the plucking," Oberon said. "You have no recognized government, no military, no weapons. But I do not believe that they will resort to such actions as long as there remains a peaceful way to prosper."

"Why not?" Aleph asked. "Why would they choose to settle peacefully with us when they could so easily take our land?"

"Trade with Carpathia is vital to them, and the Carpathians do not hold kindly to any hostile action between nations."

Aleph leaned forward in his chair and placed his arms on the table. "Get to the point, Oberon. Just where do we stand and just what is it you want us to do?"

"I want you to sail with me to Malthus," Oberon replied, clasping his hands on the table. "Vistar has requested a meeting with you. He would not do so if he were planning war. It is my guess that he wants to establish trade agreements."

"No one is going to Malthus without me," Anna stated flatly.

"I'm not sure that is wise, Anna," Oberon replied.

"He is still my father, Oberon," Anna said. "Though we have had sharp differences in the past, I may be able to influence him."

"But you were outcast!" Aleph said.

"It has been twenty years, Aleph," Oberon interrupted. "Much has changed. They no longer practice banishment and many who were outcast have returned and been welcomed back. Even Judith and Rowland have returned and now handle my affairs in Malthus."

"I wish I could be closer to Judith," Anna lamented.

"And you shall!" Oberon said with a grin. "Judith and Rowland have consented to move here and become my houselords when my estate is finished in the spring. Judith is pregnant, you know."

Anna clasped her hands to her cheeks and Aleph yielded. "Then we shall go," he replied.

Chapter 7

A Threat to Peace

A little before dawn, Aleph and Anna set out down the path toward *The Adventurer*. The warehouses were locked and vacant, the marketplace closed and empty, a fog had settled into the harbor. Aleph's legs were heavy with reluctance as his feet shuffled toward the docks. As they approached *The Adventurer*, Oberon gave them a curt greeting and they boarded.

By mid-afternoon they were well under way and Oberon was finishing his duties. Looking out over the bridge, he saw Aleph standing on the bow, leaning his head back and feeling the cool spray on his face under the hot summer sun. "Where is Anna?" Oberon asked as he approached.

"She is in our cabin napping. The last couple of days have been pretty tiring."

"You seem weary as well, Aleph."

"I am frightened, Oberon."

"Of the Star?" Oberon asked.

"No. I think I would welcome its final coming," Aleph replied. "I do not fear death so much as decisions we may have to make." He paused for a moment.

"What is he like, Oberon? I only know what Anna has told me and that has been precious little for she finds it painful to speak of him."

"Vistar? Well, he is charming and cunning, engaging and underhanded, gracious and ruthless. He is a disciple of evil clothed as the consummate diplomat. He has no conscience."

Aleph wrinkled his brow. "I expect that I will be at a great disadvantage when it comes to negotiating."

"I will be there with you, Aleph. I have known him long," Oberon said.

Aleph's sleep was restless that night, and his thoughts were troubled throughout the remainder of the voyage. When they arrived at Vistar's estate, its appearance did little to uplift Aleph's spirits. A high rock wall encircled the main house, servant quarters, stables, and a barracks which housed the Elite Guard. It was a compound of gray stone walls, streaked black by time.

A soldier met them at the gate and escorted them to the main house. Once inside, servants showed them to sleeping rooms. They refreshed themselves then met in the massive dining hall for their evening meal. Its rock floors, rock walls, and a high domed ceiling made for a cold, hollow appearance, and every sound made an echo.

Aleph was silent, pensive, deep in thought as they waited for the host. His fears were allayed somewhat when they received a warm and gracious welcome when Vistar arrived. There was feasting and entertainment, and Vistar proved a most gracious host, though he avoided Anna, ignoring her completely.

When the time came for negotiations to begin, Vistar ushered Oberon, Aleph and Anna from the banquet hall, across the atrium, and toward the library. As they walked past the guards, Vistar stopped in his tracks. "Arrest her!" he ordered.

Aleph's shock and disbelief prevented him from acting initially, but when two of the guards grasped Anna by the arms, he lost all reason and lunged toward them. Four other guards instantly poised their spears at Aleph's chest, stopping him in his tracks. Oberon grabbed the sleeve of Aleph's robe and drew him gently back.

"It would be foolhardy to resist," Vistar said as Anna was taken away. Aleph and Oberon were ushered under guard to the library, followed by Vistar. As they entered the room Vistar ordered the guards to remain outside then closed the large double doors behind him, turned and fixed his steel-gray eyes on Aleph's face. "This meeting shall be brief. I shall come directly to the point and state my position clearly. Your copper has severely damaged the demand for our flint products. Our land is growing poor and we simply cannot permit that to happen."

"What are you going to do with Anna?" Aleph asked frantically.

"She shall remain imprisoned until our negotiations are complete. If you do not agree to my terms, then I will take great pleasure in directing her torture. I assure you that she will have a slow and painful death. If my terms are met, she will be released unharmed."

Aleph stood, eyes wide, mouth open. "Surely you do not mean such things. Anna is your daughter!"

Vistar snapped a glare back at Aleph, then strode up to him and grasped him by the front of his robe. "You silly little man!" he sneered. "I have spent many hours planning ways to exact pain from her equal to the pain she has exacted from me." He pushed Aleph away as he released his grip, then turned and walked toward the window. "But I am not so stupid as to favor revenge over profit."

"But she is your own flesh and blood!"

Vistar swirled around, extended his arm and pointed his finger at Aleph, "Beware, Aleph! If we do not have our way, she will be the first to suffer my wrath, and her torture will be far more excruciating than your mousy little mind can imagine!"

Aleph started to speak again, but Oberon grasped his arm firmly, looked him in the eye and shook his head. Aleph followed Oberon's urging and silenced himself. Oberon then he turned to Vistar. "What are your terms, Vistar?" he asked.

"Who owns the mines?" Vistar asked, looking toward Oberon.

"Why, no one," Oberon replied. "No one owns the copper. They use the mountains as I use the sea."

"It is true," Aleph added. "Anyone can go into the mountains and take what they want. The copper is everywhere and there is more than enough to last lifetimes."

"I want the rights to all of it," Vistar said.

"But no-one has the right to give you those rights," Aleph replied.

"If you do not find a way to do so, my army will take your land and enslave your people to do our work."

Oberon glanced knowingly toward Aleph. "I have no doubt that your military could subdue them quickly," he said, "but you would not have invited us here if that was your intention. Just what is it you propose?"

"Aleph shall see to it that his people provide me with a boatload of copper every three moons," Vistar said. "I will see to it that his workers are paid fairly for what they deliver."

"But they do not produce that much copper," Oberon said.

"Then they must find a way," Vistar said.

"Why do you not use your own workers?" Aleph asked.

"Our people are artisans. Their talents are better spent crafting than mining. With your copper, we will make the finest tools and weapons the world has ever seen."

"And no doubt the Carpathians pay well for fine implements," Aleph added sarcastically. "You have it all figured out to get maximum production, don't you?"

Vistar shot Aleph a menacing glance. "What will your answer be, Aleph?"

"I will agree to your plan, Vistar," Aleph replied, "but only if you release Anna unharmed."

"I will release Anna when you prove to me that you can keep your part of the bargain," Vistar said. "She will be freed when the first load of copper is delivered to our shores and the Overseers have assured me that it has been delivered without interference."

"But I cannot leave without Anna!"

"Then you shall die with her here," Vistar replied, "but not before you witness the horrors I have in store for her." He turned back toward the door. "You will give me your decision by midnight," he said, as he walked out leaving Oberon and Aleph standing there alone.

"I must capitulate," Aleph said as he slumped into a chair. "What choice do I have?"

"He is a hard man, Aleph. He will not hesitate to carry out his threats."

"Well his threats have worked, Oberon," Aleph said. "I cannot let Anna come to harm, and if it means giving him the rights to our copper to save her, then so be it."

"He knows that Anna is your weakness and he will not hesitate to use her as a weapon against you, but there are larger things at stake as well. It appears to be the only thing you can do to prevent the enslavement of Oxymora."

"But how will I deliver what Vistar wishes?" Aleph asked.

"This has become an issue which affects all lands, Aleph, and I fear that you cannot achieve what you desire without a recognized government. Being a recognized government would give you audience in other lands. It would also allow you to claim the copper as a government resource."

"And how would that help?" Aleph asked.

"Your copper has made Oxymora a piece of a much larger puzzle," Oberon replied. "You no longer live in a self-sufficient society and you are especially vulnerable in matters of resources and trade. Without some kind of organized central leadership to mediate, resolve and enforce, chaos will surely erupt on a larger scale."

"But we have no real need for government," Aleph protested. "Our numbers are small and we are concerned only with the common good. We live in harmony and work together, our villages cooperate with one another, providing assigned commodities and labor. It is The Way of survival for us. We must give freely that life might sustain itself. We must give as the trees give their fruit or the flowers their pollen. We must give because there is need, nothing more. It is The Way."

"I suppose we have all tried to deny the changes which are coming about," Oberon replied, "but it is easy to see that giving up the copper will have far-reaching effects."

"I suppose you are right, Oberon," Aleph said. "I had not given much thought to how the decisions I make here will affect lives in Carpathia and Nod. I suppose it will be difficult to explain to them why they can no longer buy copper from us."

"You simply cannot manage these problems without a recognized government," Oberon said. "Even Malthus has a recognized government."

"I suppose a government is needed, for we have our own internal problems as well," Aleph admitted. "We have always taken pride in our diversity, but it is that very diversity which has created complexity. Cooperation between and among the villages is becoming increasingly difficult to achieve. Our land will soon be in need of law and leadership if it is to continue to flourish."

"And there will be continuing problems in keeping the peace with Malthus," Oberon said.

Suddenly, Vistar swung the doors open and entered the library. "It is midnight. What is your decision?"

Aleph hung his head. "You win, Vistar. What do we do from here?" he asked.

"You will meet with my money counters tomorrow and work out the details. My Overseers and a crew of laborers will return with you to Oxymora."

"I must see Anna once more before we go," Aleph said.

"Take him to her," Vistar said to his guard, then he turned and walked to the doors. "Beware, Aleph," he snarled without turning around, "if you cannot keep your end of the bargain your beloved Oxymora will see destruction you have not imagined." Then he laughed menacingly as he flung open the doors and marched haughtily from the room, robes flowing behind him.

The guards led Aleph and Oberon down through dank corridors and into Anna's dimly-lit cell. Aleph embraced her as never before, holding her tightly to him and sobbing.

"Aleph, what is it? What has my father done?"

His shoulders drooped; his arms fell to his side; his head bowed, as he squeezed one more sigh from his body. "He wanted the rights to our copper and I gave it to him."

"Is it the price you paid for my ransom?"

"I had to, Anna," Aleph replied. "You have no idea what your father might do to you."

"No, Aleph! No!" she shouted. "You cannot lay the blame for this upon me! I would have no such action taken in my name and I resent you for placing me in such a position!"

"There are other factors, Anna," Oberon said. "Your father will overthrow Oxymora and enslave its people if we do not comply with his wishes. He is holding you ransom until the first load of copper is delivered."

Aleph began sobbing again. Anna encircled his neck with her arms and soothed his brow with her fingers. They held one another for a long while. "I worry about you Aleph," she said. "I shall be all right. You must do what you must do."

"We shall meet Vistar's demands as quickly as possible, Anna," Oberon said. "You shall not stay here long."

And so it was that Oberon and Aleph returned to Oxymora without her, and Aleph brought with him a deeper admiration for Anna's strength, determination and character.

Chapter 8

A Birth and a Death

It was late fall when *The Adventurer* docked at Trada, and the piers and the marketplace buzzed with tension. Aleph had been so preoccupied with Anna's welfare that he had completely forgotten that this was the Year of the Star. Though the ominous ball of fire had not yet appeared, the possibility that its arrival might bring the final cataclysm had everyone on edge.

Nonetheless, a great crowd had gathered at the docks to greet them. News from Malthus always seemed to offer Oxymorans a sense of hope and promise, and there was no way for Aleph to avoid addressing them. He moved slowly to the side of the ship then stepped up to the railing and looked out over the crowd.

"People of Oxymora!" he began. "The Star shall come and the Star shall pass. It is not yet time for us to meet our end, so let us look to our future. With Oberon's help, we have struck a trade agreement with Malthus which will help us to prosper. I will hold a banquet this evening at the inn, and I am inviting an elder from each village to join me. There I will outline the details, and you can rest assured that our future will outshine that cursed Star."

Oberon stepped up to Aleph's side, "Let us toast prosperity and plan for our future," he said, handing Aleph a cup of wine, "and then our celebration of the passing of the Star shall be even sweeter."

Aleph lifted his cup and the crowd cheered. Turning to Oberon he said, "You always have a way of lending credibility and a sense of security to sticky situations, Oberon. I am grateful for your support."

When evening came, the inn became the center of attention as the village elders seated themselves at Aleph's table. Dinner was amiable and optimistic, and when they finished eating, Aleph began. "Welcome, my friends. I have asked you here to discuss the future of our copper trade. The demand for our copper is growing, and I fear that if we do not take control of it someone else will."

"And just how do you propose to do this?" an elder asked.

"The best way to protect our resources is to establish a recognized council government which has the power to make decisions regarding mining and distribution."

"He is right," said an elder from one of the mining camps. "Territorial disputes have already broken out and there are growing disagreements over rights and responsibilities."

"I agree," said a merchant from Trada. "There will soon come the day when a dispute is not settled, and it will spawn other disputes and those still others. We need a government to establish universal laws, rules and boundaries. We need a way to resolve intervillage conflicts, set rules for mining and trade, and see to it that there is fair distribution of profits."

"I propose that we build a central storehouse here in Trada," Aleph said. "By having the authority to manage distribution, we can command higher prices for all instead of competing with one another."

"And what do you think of the arrangement, Oberon?" another elder asked. "You have much invested in our copper trade."

"My future depends on it," Oberon replied. "It seems to me that Aleph's plan is the most feasible solution, given the circumstances."

"If it is good enough for Oberon, then it is good enough for me," the merchant from Trada called back. "He is the most cunning man I know."

They all laughed. "All right, Aleph," the elder from the mining camp said, "what do we do from here?"

"Return to your villages and urge everyone to mine as much copper as possible, as quickly as possible, then bring your copper here by the second moon. It is then that you will elect your representatives to the Council of Elders, and the level of representation you enjoy will be in direct proportion to the amount of copper you produce."

When the meeting was over, Aleph turned to Oberon. "What has happened to us, Oberon? Why is it that progress means that simple things become complex? Copper has brought us prosperity, but it has also brought its own problems."

Aleph's challenge was met with great enthusiasm. Mining the copper not only provided the people with a diversion from their fear of the Star , it gave them a sense of empowerment over their future.

When the Star appeared, it cast its brilliance over the land so that night appeared as day, but this time, instead of cursing the light, they used it to double their mining efforts. It was a minor act of defiance, and the people bonded together with a common goal. If the Star spared them once more, perhaps they could make their lives for the next twenty years a little richer, so it was with renewed purpose that the villagers brought copper to Trada in record amounts, and within two months they had delivered enough copper to fill *The Adventurer's* hold.

When the Star did pass, the election was held as promised, and Aleph had little difficulty obtaining the Council members' signatures, officially granting the rights to the copper. Their hope had been renewed, and the new government was eager to take any action which might brighten their future. So, with the last bit of the precious metal safely loaded on *The Adventurer*, Aleph and Oberon set sail for Malthus, copper rights in hand.

When they arrived in Malthus, Aleph and Oberon went directly to Vistar's estate. Upon being granted audience with Vistar, Aleph dispensed with the amenities and came straight to the point. "You have your copper and your signed agreement. Release Anna."

"Anna is not here," Vistar replied coldly as he looked over the document.

"Then where is she?" Aleph demanded. "What have you done with her?"

"When I learned she was with child, I released her," Vistar said. "She had already served her purpose. Judith and Rowland are caring for her in their home."

"Anna is pregnant?" Aleph asked as he turned to Oberon. "Take me to their home, Oberon. I must see her."

When they arrived, Anna was waiting in the doorway holding her belly and pouching it out slightly. "Hello, Aleph," she said, smiling warmly.

"Our child?" he asked, placing his hand on her abdomen.

Anna giggled. "Our voyage was a productive one indeed. Judith had a son, you know. He is nearly four months old. They named him Dunston."

Aleph just stared at her, smiling.

"Come, Aleph," she said. "Let's talk while Oberon takes care of his business with Judith and Rowland."

They strolled down the path to the garden. "Anna, let us go now before something else happens," Aleph said.

"I cannot make the voyage until after the baby is born," she replied.

"Of course! Yes, of course," he stammered, "but what has happened to you since I saw you last? Did Vistar hurt you? Are you all right? Are you safe here?"

"I spent only one night in the cell," Anna replied. "After you left my father returned me to my old room in the palace. When I learned I was pregnant, he arranged for me to move and stay with Judith and Rowland."

"That does not sound like the Vistar I dealt with," Aleph said.

"Aleph, it is all right!" she reassured him. "Go back to Oxymora and take care of business, then return here in the fall when the baby is due. There will never be anything large enough to stand between me and you for long, and there is nothing that can stand before the fulfillment of the Prophecy. With or without your permission or mine, with or without my father's interference, Oxymora will flourish and our son shall take his part in that destiny."

"A son?" Aleph asked, but he did not question further how Anna knew. And so Aleph did return once more without his beloved Anna. He went about the business of compensating the miners, heading the Council, and collecting copper, but his heart was in Malthus with Anna.

When the time for the birth drew near, Aleph sailed to Malthus as planned to be by Anna's side. It was a time of joyous reunion for Aleph and Anna. They talked and they laughed and they cried and they waited.

When Buceph was born, there was much rejoicing, for the birth symbolized a new beginning to all who knew of the Prophecy. But the birth was strenuous and difficult for Anna, and on the following day, complications overshadowed their merriment--complications the healers could not treat. Anna was dying.

When Aleph was told, a sickening panic exploded inside him. He wanted to run but Anna had summoned him to her side. As he entered her chambers, Rowland and Judith were attending her. Anna was thin, dark circles underlined her eyes, her face was pale and wan. It was obvious that she was near death, and tears filled Aleph's eyes.

Despite her weakened condition, Anna began without hesitation. "My beloved Aleph. I shall not be long in this world and there is much I need to settle before I go."

His shoulders drooped, his ears rang, his body went limp as he sank heavily into the chair which sat beside Anna's bed. She clasped his hand in hers and smiled warmly. "I know that you will grieve my passing but hold no regrets. Our lives were filled with all the things that chosen ones are allowed. There were mistakes and anger and fear, but there was also forgiveness and joy and love. Any life so lived should not be regretted."

"I was too soon smart and too late wise," Aleph replied, a tear spilling down his cheek.

"The past is past and cannot be changed but the future will be molded by decisions made here today," Anna said in a serious tone, hoping that Aleph would be able to turn his focus to the welfare of their son. "I must know that Buceph will be provided what he needs to grow healthy and strong."

Aleph was still in shock. "Yes, of course," he said flatly, "we must think of Buceph."

"What should we do about his upbringing, Aleph?"

"I don't know," Aleph replied hesitantly.

"We must decide this now," she insisted.

"It never considered that you might. . . ." His voice trailed into silence.

"That I might die, Aleph?" Anna said pointedly. "It is necessary for us to speak frankly for there is not time to play with truth."

"I know, Anna," he conceded, "it's just so hard. What am I to do? We both know that I have not the knowledge, the self-esteem, the stability to provide the things a child needs. I am hardly able to care for myself! How could I care for another?"

"For once, my beloved, we are in agreement," Anna chuckled softly and Aleph could not help but smile as well. "A child needs the things a family can provide--encouragement to nourish his creativity, dependability to foster his trust, love expressed to build his character."

Aleph nodded but did not speak.

"Judith and I have talked," Anna continued. "She and Rowland have offered to raise Buceph as their own--a son to them and a brother to Dunston."

It was not difficult for Aleph to concur. His selfishness had not so completely clouded his reason that he deluded himself into thinking that any resources he might have would be sufficient to provide the things a child would need. "Then let it be their charge," he said, looking to Judith for confirmation.

Judith nodded, choking back tears as Anna continued. "Then it is my wish that he spend his Time of Knowledge in Trada where he will learn rules and boundaries, develop his social skills, receive his formal schooling, and learn the rituals of religion. Here he can know a time of play, a time of safety, a time of love."

"And what of his Time of Reason, Anna?" Aleph asked. "Where should he go when he is twelve?"

"A young boy needs to be mothered, an older one fathered," she replied, very sure of her decision. "In Bonaventure he will begin to understand what he has learned. There he can discover the ways of law and politics and world affairs. There he can explore, adventure, discover, so that when he reaches his Time of Wisdom he will be well prepared for whatever tasks lie before him."

"I prom. . . ." Aleph caught himself before he made a foolish promise about such a serious matter. "I will be as true to your wishes as I am able," he said somberly. "I want you to know that I hear you, Anna, and I will try to be the kind of person you can count on."

Anna smiled and winked at him. Her life was fading rapidly and she held tightly to Aleph's hand. Sensing that these were Anna's last moments, Judith and Rowland quietly approached the bed. Acknowledging their presence, Anna mustered the energy for one final request. "Then these are my wishes for my son," she said, looking directly at Judith. "Be attentive when there is need, firm when there is danger, kind when there is anger, and find laughter to share."

Anna turned her gaze toward Aleph. "And to you, Aleph, be tender when there is hurt, honest when there is doubt, accepting when there are differences, and do not hurt one another with words or deeds. Then, when there is something you can do together that you both enjoy, you both shall be free to do it."

51

Judith stepped closer with tears streaming. Anna's breathing was shallow now. Her life force was slipping away. "It's paradoxical, isn't it," Anna mused, "how much closeness lies in separation. The most intimate things sometimes happen at the greatest distances." She closed her eyes for a moment, then opened them and stared at the ceiling. "When we are all children again on a different shore, let's laugh and play together," she said with a faint smile.

Her breathing stopped. They all sobbed in silence.

Chapter 9

The Lamb

Aleph stood on the Promontory Point looking down to the rocks below. He reluctantly took the crystal from around his neck, held it up to the sunlight and awaited the Guide. Within moments, the Guide beckoned to him from the trail and Aleph followed in obedient silence.

The weight of helplessness and hopelessness hung heavy upon Aleph, making the path long and arduous. Approaching the Ascetic's cave, he leaned forward over the back of the old stump chair, standing in the Ascetic's presence as if unworthy to sit. Placing his hands on the seat, he stared at the ground, sighing deeply. "Anna is dead," he said flatly, "and I am full of emptiness."

"All things, when taken away, leave the hole they once occupied," the Ascetic replied. "The larger the thing, the greater the hole. It will take much to fill it."

"And just what kinds of things can fill such a hole?"

"Simple things," the Ascetic replied. "Love, kindness, hope."

"My sadness and my regrets have crowded out such things," Aleph said. "There is only room for pain."

"If you believe that punishment is due, then take comfort in your pain," replied the Ascetic.

"Pain can be quite comforting when it is well-deserved," Aleph said.

"Embracing your regrets is a necessary part of celebrating your loss, but let your grieving end lest you fall into self-pity so you can provide yourself with a sense of justice. It is The Way of faith."

"I know The Way of faith," Aleph acknowledged, "but I have not followed it. My fear is the only thing which has remained faithful."

"You are no different from any other," the Ascetic said. "All human vessels are filled with an ever-changing blend of fear and faith, apathy and empathy, indecision and resolve, hesitation and action. It is the measure of these that will ultimately determine the depth of your failures or height of your accomplishments."

Aleph stared at the fire for a time, pondering his actions and procrastinations. "What must I do from here, Ascetic?"

"Perhaps it is time for you to go into the Dark Forest alone."

"But there are serpents awaiting those who venture there alone."

"And you must face them, for if you do not find courage now, you shall be lost in a darker place forever with serpents you cannot even imagine."

"Then I shall find The Way of courage or I shall not emerge at all." With that, Aleph bid the Ascetic goodbye and headed for the wood.

The forest was not at all what Aleph had expected. It was, in fact, quite generous and kind. There were berries and fruits and streams, and the leaf-carpeted forest floor made a very suitable bed. He spent his days wandering, meditating, evaluating his life; he spent his nights waiting for the serpents.

On the night of the first full moon, as Aleph slept, a cloud appeared over his head, and from the cloud emerged a lamb. "Who are you?" Aleph asked with a start.

"I am The Life That Is," replied the lamb.

Aleph stared at the woolly creature who now stood under a tree near his bed. "I'm not even sure I believe in The Life That Is," he said.

"My being does not depend on your believing it," said the lamb as he lay down at Aleph's feet.

"Very well," Aleph said. "If you are The Life That Is, then where were you when I needed you? I sought you but you never came."

"I have been with you always, Aleph," the lamb replied. "Because you did not recognize me does not mean I was not there--it only means that you did not recognize me."

"I did not know to look for a lamb," Aleph said.

"You see me as you see me. I appear to you as a lamb because you have called upon your Spirit of Innocence."

Aleph stared at the lamb for a moment then hung his head. "Perhaps there was a glimmer of innocence in my youth, but there is none left in me now. I have been guilty of many transgressions."

"You were guilty of nothing more than innocence," said the lamb, "and a victim of your pain."

"If you are suggesting that I did not know better, you are wrong," Aleph said. "I knew the law, I understood obedience and I recited the rituals of prayer. It's just that I have not always followed the rules."

"Many of the people who make the rules have never even played the game," replied the lamb. "I require no rituals. People require rituals to sustain their belief in magic. Rituals are born of fear and serve no purpose save to keep people under control."

"Are you saying that The Way is not about following rules? Is it not about doing right and being good?" Aleph asked.

"No, Aleph, The Way is not about doing right and being good. It is about doing what needs to be done and being kind. Much of what you were taught in your youth is about the nature of people--not about the nature of The Life That Is."

"Then why do people do good deeds in your name?"

"People do not do good deeds for me, they do good deeds for themselves and their own celebrity. It is only when they do not receive what they desire that they blame me for abandoning them."

"But are we not supposed to depend on you to fulfill our worldly needs?"

"Worldly needs are of no concern to me," the lamb replied. "If I supplied worldly things, it would be to those things that people would attribute their happiness and I would get the credit. But it would also be to their lack that they would attribute their misery, and I would get the blame. And what would I offer to those whose stomachs are full?"

"Are you saying that you are not interested in things of this world at all?"

"I am concerned only with things that are real," the lamb replied. "It is only the spiritual that matters. Things you call material are but an illusion. They are here but for an instant, then they rust or die."

"Then what have all my sacrifices gained me?" Aleph asked. "I thought that sacrifice would set me in good light with The Life That Is."

"Look at me, Aleph! I am a lamb! If I required sacrifices, do you not think that I would probably be the first on the altar? No, Aleph, I do not require sacrifice--people choose to sacrifice to affirm their goodness and prove their superiority over others."

"Perhaps I have expected much of you that you are not," Aleph said frowning.

"There are many who are disappointed when they find that I am only interested in things of the spirit," said the lamb.

"While people are interested in things material," Aleph added.

"That is where misunderstanding occurs," said the lamb. "In their innocence, they expect me to be a magician, but I do not perform tricks which bend nature and break my own laws. In their arrogance, they expect me to be their servant, but I do not indulge whims or grant wishes. In their fear, they expect me to be an extortionist, but I do not hold people for ransom demanding goodness in exchange for a future of comfort. In their greed, they expect me to be a benefactor, but I do not bestow elaborate gifts on the deserving while depriving the needy of their due. There are no material solutions to spiritual problems."

"Then why do you make it so difficult for people to understand and to find you?"

"I do not make it difficult at all," the lamb replied. "You need only to seek me where I live. I am here, and now, and living within you."

"I almost forgot my purpose for being here," Aleph said. "I did not come here to find you. I came here to face the serpents."

"Everything you came looking for, you came looking with," said the lamb. "The serpents are within you. It is yourself that you are to face."

"And what will happen if I do?" Aleph asked.

"You will find yourself, and when you do, you will know that I am The Life That Is in everyone. The creator is also the creation." With that the lamb disappeared back into the cloud.

Aleph woke with a start and quickly scrambled to his feet. Glancing nervously around the forest, he slowly sat himself down. His vision of the lamb had been so vivid--more than just a dream--yet he found himself quite alone. Dazed and confused, he huddled against the trunk of a tree, hugged his arms around his legs and stared into the darkness until dawn.

Chapter 10

A Time of Reason

In the days that followed, Aleph could not pry the vision of the lamb from his thoughts. The encounter had brought his priorities into focus, and Buceph's welfare was uppermost in his mind.

When Oberon's estate was completed in the spring, Judith and Rowland moved to Oxymora as planned, and Aleph felt a little more at ease with his baby son close at hand.

In the beginning, Aleph spent a great deal of time in Trada with Judith and Rowland, discussing, planning, preparing for Buceph's future. He intended to see to it that Anna's final wishes would be fulfilled and that his son would be well cared for.

With everything arranged, Aleph returned to Bonaventure to set about the business of picking up the pieces of his life. His visits to Trada were brief and infrequent, though he was always welcome. He watched his son grow, but usually from afar. Ever-present in the back of his mind was his pending responsibility for guiding Buceph through his Time of Reason, and he doubted he would be equal to the task.

Oberon provided well for Judith and Rowland in return for their management of his estate and business affairs, and they settled into a happy, safe, and comfortable life of domesticity in Trada. Aleph often wondered if Oberon built the estate just for that purpose. Oberon's talk of wanting a home was certainly not matched by his actions, for he was seldom there. His love of the sea would never leave him, though he did return to Trada for brief periods between adventures.

The Keeper of the Trees

The boys loved Oberon, and Oberon, this jolly rounder with the big heart, embraced and enfolded them all as if they were his own. Their fondest times were when they would all gather by the hearth to hear Oberon tell of his adventures, for he was a master story teller, and fired their imaginations with visions of foreign lands, strange customs, and unknown treasures. Listening to his tales, their heads buzzed with bright promise and their hearts were filled with laughter-laced love.

It was during Buceph's fifth year that Oberon returned from one of his adventures with a young Nodite girl, orphaned during the recent decline of that troubled land. Her name was Beth and she was four. Judith suspected that this beautiful little redhead with the freckled face was Oberon's daughter by some forgotten fling on a foreign shore, for the Nodites were dark of skin and hair, but she never questioned.

When Oberon requested of Judith and Rowland that Beth be accepted into their home, they claimed her as one of their own without question or hesitation. And so, the second generation of the House of Oberon now numbered three, each of different parentage, but kin by virtue of love.

From the very beginning, Judith and Rowland admired Beth's independence, determination and resilience, not unlike Oberon's. Beth captured the boys' hearts as well and the three of them became constant and inseparable companions, steadfast and loyal each to the other from the beginning. Together, they laughed, loved, fought and grew. They faced the same tragedies, cried the same tears, laughed the same laughter as most siblings though they were prodigious children, quick to learn and understand, and quite precocious and competitive. Together, they attended the most challenging schools, and were consistently the outstanding students in class, but while they thrived on challenges and achievements, they also took great delight in play.

They splashed in the rivers and streams, swam in the cove, ventured into the woods, and roamed the plains, seeking, learning, exploring and sneaking away to their secret place in the Elysian Wood. Here they had found a cave which was well hidden by dense foliage growing atop the steep wall of the river gorge. It was quiet and peaceful, save for the hypnotic roar of the river below, and they were safe, here they were free, and it was here that they dreamed their dreams.

As Buceph's twelfth year approached, Judith called him to her side. "My beloved son," she began, "you are fast approaching your Time of

Reason and, with its coming, you must embark on a new adventure. It was ordained long ago that you spend your Time of Knowledge here with us, but that your Time of Reason should be spent with your father in Bonaventure. Though this will be difficult for all of us, and especially for you, this must be in order to make your heritage meaningful and your Time of Wisdom complete."

"But I hardly know my father," Buceph protested in disbelief. "You have told me much of him, but I have only known occasional brief visits with a stranger. And besides, everyone says that my father is a troubled man. They speak of his aloneness, and I fear that I will be alone as he is alone."

"And that is precisely why this must be," Judith replied. "Perhaps the reason your father keeps his distance from the world is that he is about business which is not of this world. The doing of loftier deeds leaves little room for earthly bonds, and thus he does not relate well to those things that we often think matter."

"Just what things *do* matter?" Buceph asked angrily.

"I only know that his purpose and the legacy he shall leave to you are part of a great plan," Judith replied. "The Ascetic gave your father a Prophecy many years ago--a promise of hope and purpose. Part of that Prophecy is that Oxymora is to be a haven for the lost. Your father's purpose is to make a home for those who are lost. It is a purpose you shall inherit and it matters very much."

"What does the rest of the Prophecy say?" Buceph asked.

"It says that from the House of Aleph shall descend the Keeper of the Trees."

"What is the Keeper of the Trees?" Buceph asked.

"No one fully understands that, Buceph, but it has to do with one who will fulfill our promise of hope for the future."

Buceph was thoughtful for a moment. "But I do not wish to leave this, my home, for another."

"Nor do I want you to go, my son," replied Judith wistfully, "but there is a destiny to be served which is greater than the wishes of you or me. I think it is not for us to understand, but I feel deep with me that it is ours to do."

"But all my friends are here," he continued to protest. "What of Beth and Dunston? I shall miss them greatly."

"Buceph, you have been chosen for a noble cause, one for which you are well suited, for I have seen the great pride you take in this land, your deep love for it, your powerful desire to protect and nourish it," Judith soothed.

After a brief period of sulking silence, Buceph acquiesced, though it angered him deeply to be torn from the only family he had ever known. "Then I shall go, and if it does not destroy me, perhaps it will strengthen me," he said.

Buceph's twelfth year was the worst in his short life. Compared to his boyhood home, his new life at Bonaventure was nearly unbearable. He missed Dunston and Beth gravely. Overnight, his emotions had been catapulted from the carefree joys of youth into the glum boredom of responsible adulthood, and he grieved the childhood he had left behind in the House of Oberon.

Bonaventure was a very adult place indeed. Children were scarce, for most who frequented Bonaventure had homes and families in more playful places. To Buceph, the leaders were seriously absorbed in the excitement of power, politics, philosophy and religion. Everything about this place was strictly business; lighthearted moments were exceedingly rare.

Though Bonaventure offered great potential for new challenges, adventures, and discoveries, Buceph was haunted by the warmth and laughter of his childhood home. Night after night, he silently cried himself into an exhausted sleep.

To make matters worse, Buceph's darkest images of his father were coming true, and no more than two weeks had passed before they had their first confrontation.

"Why am I here, father?" Buceph asked one night over dinner.

Aleph set down his utensil and, placed his elbows on the table, clasping his hands and placing his pointed fingers on his chin. "If you must know, it is to satisfy your mother's dying wish," he replied flatly.

"Then you do not wish me here any more than I wish to be here?" Buceph asked.

Aleph fidgeted, dropping his hands into his lap. "I shall always care about you, for you are my son. I shall always care what happens to you, for you are destined to play a part in the Prophecy. Unfortunately, I do not know how to translate that caring into parenthood."

"My mother told me about the Prophecy, but I do not understand it. What are the Trees and what is their Keeper supposed to do?"

"I wish I could tell you, my son. I only know what the Ascetic has told me--that the Keeper of the Trees is one who shall bring The Way of freedom to the world."

"And what are the Trees?" Buceph asked.

"The Ascetic said that I would never know them, but that they represent gratitude, and joy, and forgiveness. They offer love and humility and faith and life itself."

Buceph was quiet for a time. "I think it fair to tell you that I resent having been sentenced to your care," he said, sulking slightly.

"And I to your upbringing," Aleph replied.

Buceph was taken aback. Feeling attacked, he responded angrily. "Is that why you leave me to the care of the housekeepers? Is that why you do not spend time with me? Is that why you devote all your waking hours to the duties of your office?"

Aleph hung his head for a moment then looked out the window. "Have you arranged your schedule?" he asked, avoiding Buceph's barrage of questions.

"Your Aid has arranged it for me," Buceph said as he threw his utensils on the table and stomped from the room.

From that day forward, Buceph observed his father closely, partly because of lack of trust, and partly because of curiosity about Aleph's position.

During his second year in Bonaventure, Buceph began secretly following Aleph to the Council Chambers and eavesdropping on affairs of state. After one such session when the Council was discussing the Malthusian issue, Buceph felt compelled to confront his father for the second time, and at dinner that evening, Buceph seized his opportunity. "Father, we dine together each evening, and yet I know little of the affairs you deal with each day."

"Affairs of state are not your concern," Aleph replied. "You will have concerns over them soon enough. Do not rush yourself, Buceph."

Buceph continued eating for a time then went on. "I was in the Council Chambers today."

Aleph continued eating and made no reply.

"I overheard the discussion about the Malthusians. What are you going to do about them?"

"That is up to the Council, it is not up to me."

"But you are the one who struck the agreement with them," Buceph insisted.

"And I intend to do no more," Aleph replied.

"You are afraid of them, aren't you?" Buceph prodded. "You are afraid to take any action against them. Why?"

Aleph returned to eating his meal, avoiding Buceph's question entirely.

"Father, I have been sneaking into the Council Chamber for some time now, and I think you are afraid to make *any* decisions. The Council does whatever it pleases, and all you ever do is nod your head in agreement. You never offer a dissent, never an argument--you never even offer an opinion. It seems to me you are a leader being led."

"I do what I must," was Aleph's only reply.

The more Buceph came to understand his father's fear, the more he blamed Aleph for Oxymora's problems, and a deep anger began to lurk within him. He grew resentful of his father's inaction and indecision, for he knew that Aleph's position carried great influence, yet he refused to exert that influence to make changes for the better.

Buceph was angry. He was angry at the illusion which was being shattered, angry at the fear which prevented his dreams from being fulfilled, and angry at having been left alone. He spent the remainder of his time in Bonaventure avoiding any kind of interaction with Aleph. He was obsessed with the notion that fear would not control him as it had his father, yet all the while he feared that it might, and thus it did.

Upon his eighteenth birthday, Buceph was preparing to embark upon his Time of Wisdom. He had served his time and was eager to leave his father's house behind and return to Trada to rejoin his companions--to go back home. He had not seen them in six long years and his heart longed for that missing piece of himself.

When the hour came for Buceph to depart, Aleph was busy with another newcomer. The time for Buceph's departure came and went, and Buceph's departure went unnoticed. Hurt and dismayed, Buceph intended this to be the final insult his father would ever inflict upon him, and he vowed that he would not return to Bonaventure until Aleph's dying day.

The Elder of Trada brought the news to Dunston and Beth that Buceph would soon return home, and they eagerly headed toward Bonaventure to meet him on the road to make his journey a little less lonely. As they spied him in the distance, Dunston shouted warmly, "Welcome home my brother. You have been well missed."

"And I have missed Trada and everyone there," replied Buceph wistfully as they approached one another, grinning broadly. The three of them embraced long and hard with tears of joyous reunion brimming over their eyes. They had much catching up to do, and they chattered incessantly as they walked along together.

Judith and Rowland held a grand feast celebrating Buceph's return, and it seemed to Buceph that everyone he had ever known attended. Even Oberon delayed *The Adventurer's* departure in order to give Buceph a proper welcome home. It was a happy time, and all hurt and anger were laid aside for a brief while.

In the days that followed, Buceph began to relax in the peaceful atmosphere of the Elysian Wood. It was a great relief being away from the seriousness and intensity of Bonaventure and he began to focus his thoughts on planning for the future. Being reunited with Dunston and Beth had restored his spirit.

They were alive with wonder and filled with a multitude of idealized notions. The authoritarian constraints which had lain upon them through their formative years had now been removed; their individual destinies were about to unfold.

Chapter 11

A Decision is Made

Aleph, alone now, immersed himself in a cloud of doom. He continued his life as best he knew though the pain of loneliness so consumed him that he became a virtual recluse. Guilt clouded his reason and the more he ruminated, the more depressed he became over the long succession of pain-strewn disasters which trailed him.

His agreement with Malthus had proven to be one of the greatest mistakes of his life. Oxymora was no longer the self-sufficient society it had started out to be. The copper which had lured so many to her shores no longer held any promise for Oxymora's people. The riches they had envisioned belonged to Malthus now, and the Oxymoran workers had become little more than a colony of ants providing to queen Malthus. Their hard work barely sustained them while the Malthusians profitted from their work. The people felt betrayed, and they blamed Aleph for their plight.

Aleph rarely showed his face in public now. He knew what he had done to his people, and he knew how much they resented him. He was a leader who lived in fear of the people he led. He refused to give audience to anyone, chores went untended, business went ignored. Every task seemed a drudgery, every breath a sigh, every movement an effort. He was withering away little-by-little, day-by-day, punishing himself with deprivation of food and sleep. He spent his days just sitting on the veranda, eyes fixed to the horizon, and he rocked, rocked, rocked. Each evening, he would go to the Promontory Point and stare at the rocks below, thinking how easy it would be to just topple over the edge and end his torment.

He thought often of returning to the Ascetic, but was too afraid to face him with nothing but failure. It all came to a head one evening when Aleph made his decision to jump. Moving to the edge of the precipice, Aleph turned to take one last look at the land he loved, but as he turned, he lost his footing and fell.

Whether by chance, by fate, or by divine intervention, a narrow ledge just below the precipice interrupted Aleph's fall. He lay there for a moment, curled in a fetal position, eyes tightly closed, hugging himself with both arms. As he slowly opened his eyes, the crystal was laying directly in his face. He scrambled to a sitting position, grasped the crystal with both hands and held it high, tears streaming down his face.

Within seconds, a hand reached down and grabbed Aleph by the scruff of his robe and jerked him upward, back to the precipice where he had stood moments before. It was the Guide.

No words were spoken between them, and Aleph's journey to the Ascetic was not without reluctance. He felt strangely like a child caught misbehaving and about to face his punishment.

As Aleph had expected, the old man was sitting quietly by the fire, but the Ascetic did not look as old as Aleph remembered. Aleph was aging, while the kindness, empathy, and understanding shined fresh in the Ascetic's timeless face.

Aleph eased himself into the stump chair, clasped his hands in his lap and leaned forward, staring at the ground. "I have come to you to confess the latest in the series of failures which is my life," he began. "Buceph has embarked upon his Time of Wisdom with much bitterness in his heart. I offered him all the opportunities I could offer, but he found me disappointing."

"People do not learn from what you provide or from what you teach, they learn from what you are," the Ascetic said.

Aleph looked up, tears filling his eyes. "Then I suppose I should not be surprised," he said. "I never knew how to relate to Buceph. He always saw me as aloof, uncaring and invulnerable."

"And being vulnerable might lead to another involvement and another involvement to another rejection?" the Ascetic asked.

Aleph's affirmation lay in his silence. He gazed at the eastern horizon. "I have been thinking a great deal about Anna lately," he reflected. "I denied her my vulnerability as well. I seldom showed her my laughter for fear of appearing foolish; I seldom showed her my tears for fear of appearing weak."

"I see," the Ascetic said. "The problem is, denying your weaknesses for fear of making yourself vulnerable sets you above everything that is human. Putting yourself in such a high place has left you lonely."

Aleph's gaze returned to the Ascetic's face. "I had never looked at it quite that way," he said. "I thought I simply preferred to remain without rather than risk the loss of something I might gain."

"It is only because you fear being alone that you are alone, but fear cannot be conquered by fear and loneliness cannot be conquered alone."

"But what if I risk involvement and lose again? I do not believe that I could survive another such failure."

"The only real failure lies in risking nothing; the only real success lies in doing."

Aleph drew his gaze inquisitively back to the old man's face then sat thoughtfully for a moment before he continued. "I suppose you are right," he admitted. "I certainly regret the things I have failed to do far more than the things I have done. The opportunities I have missed far outweigh the mistakes I might have made, and yet I still fear making mistakes."

"It is fear that causes what you fear, for inaction is also failure," replied the Ascetic. "Fear of failure has caused you to avoid success, fear of despair has caused you to avoid hope, fear of loss has caused you to avoid gain. Indeed, fear of death has caused you to avoid life."

Aleph sighed and looked back toward the horizon. "I cannot remember ever being without fear. I believe it has been with me always. I strive to keep it covered with blankets of noise and yet it lurks there, deep within me, stalking my thoughts, thwarting my decisions. I do not know how to win this silent battle."

"Your fear has only the power you give it by denying that it exists," the Ascetic said.

"But I am afraid of revealing my fear."

"Do you not realize that being afraid of revealing your fear *is* revealing your fear?" the Ascetic asked. "No, Aleph, the only way to conquer fear is to embrace it--that is the most courageous act of all."

"But if I embrace my fear, will I not continue to fail?" Aleph asked.

"The will to succeed can only be found *after* you find the courage to fail," the Ascetic replied. "Anyway, did you not seek me because you already are a failure?"

"Why, yes, that's true," Aleph replied. "I *have* already failed. I have left my future behind; the past is all I have to look forward to."

"Then you have nothing to fear," the Ascetic said, "and with nothing to fear you are free to embrace your failure as well."

"But why should I embrace failure?" Aleph asked.

"Because in your failure lies your success."

"Being a successful failure is hardly my idea of success," Aleph replied.

The Ascetic chuckled. "Then you still do not see the value of failure," he said. "Without failure there can be no challenge, without challenge there can be no purpose, without purpose there can be no success. When you embrace your failure, you will transcend your fear. When you give up your fear, you will know success."

"I sometimes think that I shall never learn from my failures," Aleph said.

"The day that you learn from them has not come yet, but it will. It will come when you are willing to give up your fear."

"Why would I be afraid of giving up my fear?"

"To give up your fear means you must also give up indifference, indecision, and hesitation," the Ascetic replied.

"Will I also give up my mistakes?"

The Ascetic chuckled again. "No, but if you make the right mistakes you will be rewarded by the appropriate failure. If you have the right kind of failures, you will be shown The Way to success."

"And if I do succeed?" Aleph asked.

"Then you will be able to endure that success because of your failures, you will endure comfort because of your pain, you will endure joy because of your sadness, you will endure victory because of your defeat."

Aleph was thoughtful for a time. "Is it my fault that the rProphecyhas gone awry, Ascetic?"

"What leads you to believe that the Prophecy has gone awry?"

"Have you not seen what is happening?" Aleph asked. "Our prosperity is dwindling, our freedoms have been infringed, our land has become a rapist's quarry. This is hardly a place of welcome for anyone."

"Things seen as today's failures are often tomorrow's successes," the Ascetic said, "just as today's villains are tomorrow's hero; today's fool tomorrow's genius."

"I suppose the reverse is also true," Aleph said. "The people of Oxymora once praised me for their gains but now they blame me for their losses."

"There is a fine line between praise and blame," the Ascetic acknowledged. "It is as changeable as the wind."

"But I am neither their solution nor their problem. I have lain no opinions before them, taken no stands, risked no decision, and yet they hold me responsible for all that is wrong."

"Perhaps inaction is the focus of their blame," the Ascetic said. "Anger is often directed not so much at what has been done, but rather at what has not been prevented."

"I would like to stand up to the Malthusians," Aleph said, "but if I do, we might lose all."

"When little of value remains, risking all is risking little."

"But what if I assert my influence and the people think my judgment poor; my actions foolish; my causes unjust?" Aleph asked.

"Could that be worse than having them believe you ignorant, cowardly, and prejudiced?" the Ascetic asked. "Is it worse than admitting that you have no mind of your own by letting others do the thinking for you?"

"But to lay my dreams before others is to risk ridicule," Aleph replied. "I could not withstand such suffering, such sorrow and loss."

"When you hold your dreams, risking nothing, you have nothing, do nothing, and are nothing," the Ascetic said.

"But what of the adversity I might encounter?"

"Success can only follow a victory, and victory can only be achieved when there is adversity," the Ascetic replied. "Without obstacles to overcome, there can be no victory."

Aleph frowned and bit nervously on his lip. "I looked to people and to circumstances to calm my fears, to ignite my passions, to light my direction, but they had not the power to provide these things."

"It is only then that you will stop hurting others."

"I am hurting no one but myself," Aleph protested.

"That is what you would like to believe," the Ascetic said, "but you always hurt others when you do not take care of yourself."

"I do not understand," Aleph said. "How can I hurt others by hurting myself?"

"When you do not take care of yourself, others are left to take care of you," the Ascetic replied. "When they try to help you, you feel unworthy and drive them away, then when they have gone, you blame them for your loneliness."

"I wish to hurt no one," Aleph said. "What must I do to make things right?"

"There is only one thing you can do," the Ascetic replied. "Accept that you are powerless. Then when you understand why you are powerless, you can choose to reclaim your strength."

"That is very confusing, Ascetic," Aleph said.

"It is really quite simple," the Ascetic said. "You give people the power to make you feel safe or threatened, content or angry, happy or sad. You give possessions the power to make you feel secure or insecure, successful or inadequate, important or insignificant. You give the past the power to make you feel guilt and the future the power to make you afraid. When you give all these things power, are you not left powerless?"

"Why yes, that's true," Aleph replied. "I had not looked at it quite that way. The more power I give to things outside myself, the less power I have, and the weaker I become."

"That is especially disconcerting when you still place your faith only in your own power."

"It has been a long time since I have had faith in anything else," Aleph admitted.

"The Life That Is offers all the power you need," the Ascetic said. "Look deep within yourself, for it is only there that you will find it. It has never left you, and now that you can embrace your own weakness, you will be able to use its power."

"It is The Way of faith, and I fear that my faith is lacking," Aleph said.

"It is the way of power," the Ascetic countered. "When you accept that things outside yourself are not responsible for your plight and stop blaming them, you will have the power to accept your responsibility and act accordingly. It is action that makes faith real."

Aleph hung his head and stared at the ground. "It is no longer important what happens to me, is it Ascetic?"

The Ascetic smiled and nodded knowingly. "It never was."

Chapter 12

A Change of Heart

The following morning, a confident Aleph strolled into the Council Chambers and announced that he would exercise his power of proclamation. There would be a new decree, the first to be made since Aleph gave their copper rights to the Malthusians. The decree would be given with the coming of the new moon.

Word of the proclamation spread quickly, and when the time drew near, Carpathia, Nod and Malthus sent representatives, and people from all corners of Oxymora journeyed to Bonaventure to witness this historic event. Every one of any importance was there--everyone except Buceph.

Aleph was visibly disconcerted by Buceph's conspicuous absence, for this decree would shape Buceph's future, the future of Oxymora, the future of the Prophecy. Could his anger be so great that he would shirk his duty, avoid his destiny? How could he remain at the Elysian Wood through an event of such importance?

Nonetheless, Aleph appeared on the steps of the temple at the appointed time and the crowd went silent as he began his pronouncement. "We of Oxymora have long known that the Malthusians are feasting on the heart of our prosperity, but everyone is afraid to say so for fear of tipping a most delicate balance."

There was an audible rustling through the crowd as the Malthusian contingent reacted vehemently to Aleph's statement, but Aleph continued undaunted. "They have slithered their way into our society and have stolen our dreams by their intrusion. They have stripped us of our resources and of our dignity until we now suffer the same timeworn problems we once would not abide. They sit in our court and study our vulnerabilities, ever alert to new ways of capitalizing on our weaknesses. Their vigilance knows no complacency."

Cheers arose from the downtrodden Oxymorans while the Malthusian contingency listened in stern silence. "Because of the Malthusians, corruption infests our government, greed splinters our unity, laws and protocols restrict our freedoms, and our allegiances have been hawked for personal gain. What was intended as a haven for the Outlanders has become the very thing from which it once offered refuge. We have become what we once despised; we have become what we once fled."

The politicians sat dumbfounded, for they had never heard Aleph assert himself quite so boldly. They could hardly applaud Aleph with their hands in the back pockets of the Malthusians. They could not oppose him without admitting their subversion, nor could they support him for fear of losing favor with the Malthusians.

"No longer shall we allow the rape of our homeland," Aleph continued. "I hereby proclaim that Oxymora rescinds all agreements with Malthus. We shall henceforth reclaim all rights to our copper. Furthermore, Malthusian diplomats shall no longer be welcomed in our Council Chambers. And if this decree makes any land our enemy, then so be it. It is decreed, let it be done." With that, Aleph turned smartly and marched proudly back into his chambers.

Suddenly unwelcome in Oxymora, the Malthusian diplomats wasted no time. Before an hour had passed, they had hastened aboard their skiffs and were sailing swiftly homeward.

When news of Aleph's proclamation reached Oberon a day later, Oberon was livid. He boarded *The Adventurer* at Trada and sailed around the western coast to Aleph's Cove. There, he disembarked and stomped through the streets of Bonaventure, yelling Aleph's name at the top of his voice.

Aleph was in the Council Chambers when he heard Oberon's bellowing. Walking out onto the balcony, he spotted Oberon coming through the square, and Oberon spotted him. Aleph had never seen his old friend so enraged.

Oberon stood there in the public square, fists firmly planted on his hips, screaming up toward Aleph's high perch. "I have worked for years to maintain a delicate balance between Malthus and Oxymora, and you have destroyed it all with a few impulsive and ill-thought-out words."

"I only did what I thought best for Oxymora." Aleph said calmly. "You know that, Oberon."

"All you have done is ensure that Oxymora will have the best funeral any land has ever had! You must come with me to Malthus! You must reverse what you have done!"

"I shall not change my mind, Oberon," Aleph said. "You can rave to your heart's content, but I shall not change my mind."

Oberon glared at Aleph. This was the first time Aleph had defied Oberon's suggestion, and Oberon was furious, but he quickly saw that Aleph's position was immutable. Oberon scowled, turned on his heels and stomped away.

Aleph smiled to himself. He was free.

After two weeks at sea, Oberon arrived in Malthus and hastened directly to Vistar's chambers. There he requested an audience, but did not receive his usual welcome. An hour passed, and no response. "Surely he will extend me the courtesy of an audience," he thought. Just then, Vistar appeared at the archway to the portico. "Hello Oberon," he said flatly. "Why the unscheduled visit?"

"Sir, we are old friends. Together we have controlled much power, made great fortunes, built much trust. I implore you to take no drastic action against Oxymora--not just yet."

"I understand that you are concerned about your interests there," Vistar said coldly. "Perhaps that is where all your loyalties lie as well."

"It is true that my estate is there," Oberon said, "but I owe allegiance to no land. I try to serve all lands equally, even if it is only to serve my own interests."

"Aleph has given me no choice," Vistar said. "We have nothing left to lose if we take Oxymora by force, and if it affects you and your trade, then I am sorry."

"Let me talk to Aleph," Oberon pleaded. "I can straighten things out. You will have your copper back. I just need a little time."

"You are too late Oberon. I have already dispatched our armadas. They sailed from the North Port this morning and will be in Oxymora by the new moon," Vistar replied icily as he sneered, turned and casually strolled away.

Oberon hung his head in sorrow. Vistar could not stop what had been wrought even if he wanted.

Chapter 13

A Time of War

They came at dawn, simultaneously invading Trada and Bonaventure, Oxymora's two most influential yet vulnerable points. The Malthusians were swift, efficient and vicious. At Trada they plundered the warehouses, confiscating foodstuffs, commodities and copper. They leveled the marketplace and burned homes, slaughtering and maiming without regard for humanity.

From Oberon's estate on the edge of town, Judith and Rowland could hear the screams from the marketplace, they could see the billowing smoke rising from the warehouses, they could smell the stench of burning flesh.

"Look, Rowland!" Judith shrieked. "There are people running from the soldiers, women and children and old men. They are running our way!"

Rowland grabbed a sickle for a weapon and burst out the door, running toward the horror and confusion.

"No Rowland!" Judith screamed, but it was too late. Rowland ran past the fleeing crowd and engaged the line of soldiers with all that was in him, but they numbered more than fifty. He felled three before being run through with a spear.

Judith screamed, then panicked and ran from the house toward him. All around her, soldiers were slashing and stabbing, slaughtering everyone in their path, but Judith could see only her dying Rowland. Struggling through the mass of chaos to reach her beloved, a soldier's spear ripped through her just as she was about to touch him and she fell at his side.

At Bonaventure, the Malthusian objective was to throw the government into chaos by eliminating the Council of Elders, and the scene there was not much different from that at Trada. A hundred soldiers made short work of virtually destroying the capital city. Every shop was razed, every public building was plundered and set ablaze, every private residence was pillaged and destroyed. The soldiers indiscriminately annihilated all who crossed their path.

Terror choked the breath from Aleph as he realized what was happening. The Council Chambers were burning, and the smoke drove him into the courtyard. Choking, dazed and confused, he staggered into the street. He was suddenly surrounded by madness, moaning, death. He clenched his fists, lifted his arms and screamed, "Kill *me*! *I'm* the one you're after! Leave *them* alone! Kill *me*! Kill *me*!"

From the smoke, a lone soldier appeared, looking to Aleph almost like an apparition. Coolly, calmly, and with a clear objective, the soldier took Aleph by the arm, almost gently, and, looking him directly in the eye, he plunged his dagger deep into Aleph's chest. Then, as quickly as he had appeared, the soldier turned and disappeared back into the smoke.

Aleph fell. Blackness. Then, there were hands all around him. He was being lifted! He was being carried! The Great Temple! It was still standing! The hands lay him in one of the fire-hollowed rooms where others had been brought to die. All around there was crying, moaning, wailing.

As quickly as they had come, they were gone, leaving behind a mass of chaos, confusion, and suffering. Of the few who were spared, some wandered aimlessly amid the rubble, some searched anxiously for loved ones, others just sat and stared, oblivious to their surroundings. When the shock wore off, there was scurrying; scurrying for food and shelter like rats in a trash heap, pride and dignity pushed aside by the urge to survive.

At the Elysian Wood, Beth was humming to herself as she prepared breakfast while Buceph and Dunston still slept. Her morning ritual was suddenly interrupted when she spotted billows of black smoke rising from the north. "Buceph! Dunston!" she screamed as she ran back into the cave. "Trada is burning! Get up! Get up!"

Buceph and Dunston jumped to their feet and sleepily tried to make sense of Beth's ranting. Exiting the cave, they saw the darkened north sky. "Something is terribly wrong," Buceph said. "We must go and see what has happened."

Gathering a few essential items, they stuffed their packs and set out immediately for Trada. Pulses quickened with their steps as they anxiously approached, then a great sinking feeling gripped them as they topped the hill and saw their beloved village reduced to smoldering rubble.

Frantic to find their parents, they followed the swath of destruction to the House of Oberon, then looked in horror at the devastation which lay before them. Their childhood home had been obliterated. Nothing was spared.

Stupefied, they began sifting through the rubble. Then Buceph let out a cry of enraged anguish as he stumbled upon the charred bodies of Judith and Rowland.

They lovingly buried their parents on the hillside overlooking the bay, then they turned their thoughts to Bonaventure. If Trada had been attacked, it was reasonable to assume that Bonaventure had been invaded as well, so they set out to assess the destruction there.

As they made their way to the House of Aleph, they expected to find him as they had found Judith and Rowland, but his house was untouched. Its distance from the hub of activity had apparently left it undiscovered, but there was no sign of Aleph.

Returning to the village, Buceph stopped everyone he saw, asking if they knew of the fate of his father. Most were so consumed with their own shock, grief, and survival that they were oblivious to the wanderings and of those around them. "Try the Great Temple," a surviving Elder finally suggested. "There are many wounded there. The healers and the priests are caring for them as best they can. If he is yet alive, he may be there."

The makeshift hospital was filled with misery and death. They wandered among the moaning wretches, searching for a familiar face. Then, in the far corner of a small room reserved for the dying, they found Aleph lying inanimate on a mat soaked in his own blood. His lips were cracked from thirst, his eyes were cloudy and dim, the life was slipping from his body.

As Buceph knelt at his father's side, there was but a faint glimmer of life remaining. "You must not die, father!" he pleaded through angry tears. "You must complete what you have begun. You created this chaos, and it is not fair for you to leave it to me to repair!"

Aleph opened his eyes and looked into his son's face. "You hold much anger toward me, and I cannot blame you for your wrath, but only death survives now, my son," he replied weakly. "As of this day, you shall receive the legacy I leave you, and it carries with it grave responsibility."

Aleph paused, laboriously gasping a few breaths of air while Buceph patiently held his father's hand, saying nothing. "Today, you shall inherit both things unwanted and things desired. As of this day, the leadership of the land is yours, and with it, all that I have gathered. The only things I shall take with me are the things I have given away; all that I have acquired shall remain with you."

Buceph's anger softened as he came to the full realization that his father was dying. A tear spilled onto his cheek. "I have been preparing myself through my youth that I might be equal to this day, but I did not imagine it to be so soon."

Aleph smiled. "I have watched you grow, my son, and I take great pride and great envy in your accomplishments, for you have achieved things I had not the courage to try. And now you shall be in a position to lead, to make this land that which the Prophecy intended it to be--vibrant and strong, productive and bountiful, just and merciful." He took Buceph's hand and looked into his face. "Have we not both dreamed of this?"

Buceph smiled warmly at his father. "True enough! I hold great hopes and great vision for this land. That, I think, is the only thing we have ever shared. I have seldom agreed with your motives and methods, but we have never been apart when it came to our dreams and aspirations."

Aleph sighed and looked around the room at the suffering and death. "The things we believe usually lie beyond the way we behave, just as the things we dream usually lie beyond the things we attain."

Buceph wiped the tear from his cheek, straightened himself, and cleared his throat. "The Malthusians have struck us a deadly blow. I fear that we have been beaten into submission. What am I to do with such a legacy, father?"

"Alas, what you say is true," Aleph admitted. "I leave you a legacy of failure, but all great things once wore failure's guise."

"Our homeland has been left weak and helpless because of your failures," Buceph replied, his anger seeping through.

Aleph was silent for a moment, smiling, not wishing to antagonize his son's hurt. "When you are able to see beyond, you will understand that the failures I leave you shall become your greatest assets, for they shall fuel your fires."

"But look to the burden you leave me to bear," Buceph retorted indignantly.

"Life's greatest burden is to have no burden to bear," Aleph replied. "I have left you many great gifts which you cannot yet see; challenges, passions, purpose; these are the things you will need in order to accomplish your goals."

"It is the Malthusians who hold our destiny now," Buceph said hopelessly, staring bitterly at the misery around him. "They have taken our land and along with it, our hope."

Aleph faded momentarily, then gasped once again for air. "It has been told to me by the Ascetic that success can only follow a victory, and it befalls you to achieve that victory. There is much for you to conquer, and your path shall be fraught with danger. You will be the one with the courage to act. I sought it all my life, but. . . ." Aleph gasped for air again. "Alas, it was only when I had nothing left to lose that I found it."

Buceph pursed his lips and squared his shoulders. "Then I shall face my enemy without fear and I shall be victorious," he said with firm resolve. "I know my task, and I shall give my all to succeed."

Aleph gasped again and grasped Buceph's arm. "And if I cannot find the courage, then have the decency to stand aside. Progress is a process, my son. I have added my piece, you shall add yours, and others theirs until the picture takes on meaning, but the puzzle shall not be complete until the final piece has been put into place."

Buceph did not fully comprehend what his father was trying to tell him, but he did not wish to belabor or bedevil his dying. "I shall not disgrace the House of Aleph, father. I shall not fail."

"I spent my life trying to avoid failure," Aleph lamented in a whisper. "I did not know that avoiding failure had nothing to do with ensuring success." Aleph's consciousness faded; his eyes closed; his breathing stopped momentarily, then resumed. Opening his eyes weakly, he continued. "I found The Way for myself, and you must find The Way for you, for mine cannot be yours, nor yours mine. Success can only follow a victory. You are entering your Time of Wisdom and you are lost." He heaved another breath into his lungs. "Take the crystal from around my neck, go to the Promontory Point and hold it high above your head. A being known as the Guide will come to you. Follow him. He will lead you to the

Ascetic. Heed the Old One's words, for they have truth and will give you direction."

Aleph closed his eyes, his breathing stopped for the final time. A man of peace had died of violence, and Buceph wept over all that he had lost and all that he had gained.

Chapter 14

From Fear to Rage

As Buceph made preparations for Aleph's burial, his anger rose with each thrust of his shovel and he began to weep. His weeping soon turned to deep sobs of frustrated rage as his father's dying words flooded his brain--*success can only follow a victory*--and silently, he vowed to exact revenge.

The Malthusians were ever-present now, forcing order upon the Oxymoran people. Malthus had forfeited their trade with Carpathia because of their aggressive action, but they had gained a land full of resources and a lot of slaves. Oxymora had been beaten into submission, and it would take nothing short of a miracle to bring these downtrodden people together as a unified nation, capable of reclaiming freedom and dignity.

Buceph, Beth and Dunston remained at Bonaventure for a time, moving cautiously and inconspicuously through the streets, not wishing Buceph's identity to be known for fear of further reprisal. They watched and they listened, learning all they could about the Malthusians' vulnerabilities.

Two weeks passed, and it became apparent that they could accomplish little in Bonaventure, so they retreated to the Elysian Wood. Dusk was approaching and a gentle rain was falling as they slopped through the mud toward home. By the time they reached the cave they were all exhausted, but Buceph's drawn face and dark-circled eyes concerned his companions greatly. His burden was heavy indeed, and the responsibilities recently placed upon his shoulders had exacted a heavy toll.

Buceph staggered to the far side of the cave, fell into his bed roll and curled up on his side. Too exhausted to eat or to speak, he just lay there, hugging himself. Feeling safe for the first time in many days, he quickly fell into a sound and restful sleep.

He did not awake until the sun was well over the horizon. Propping himself up on one elbow, he peered across the room at Beth who was stirring something over the open fire at the mouth of the cave. She had been moving about quietly so as not to disturb his deep rest and Buceph felt warm and comforted in the presence of his trusted companions. He lay back and closed his eyes again, grateful for his sense of safety.

They all needed time to heal from the traumas they had experienced recently, and each in their own way dealt with their grief. They shared their pain openly and freely, and in their mourning together, felt closer to one another than ever before. Little was spoken of their plans during the next several days. They all sensed that they could not get on with the business at hand until their sorrow had been laid to rest.

By the time a month had passed they had grieved their losses into bearability and with each passing day, Buceph's restless anger evolved into a relentless rage. He had taken to spending his days pacing angrily by the stream trying to dissipate his pent-up rage.

It was Dunston who finally brought things to a head one evening over dinner. "We have been here for more than a month now, and we have not talked of many things which matter. You have spoken little of the years you spent with your father, and nothing of our future."

"I missed so much during the time I spent in my father's house," Buceph said. "It was a bitter time and he was a worthless man."

"But all of Oxymora held your father in high regard," Beth said. "Look at the people he helped, the kindnesses he did, the friends made."

"He helped only himself, gave kindness only to be rewarded in kind and made friends only because he feared enemies," replied Buceph.

"Perhaps your vision of your father was cloudy because of your distance from him," Beth suggested.

"To the contrary," Buceph replied, "my vision was clearer because of my closeness to him. Those who were not close to him saw only the bright shades of his surface. I saw the darkness of his soul."

"Perhaps you are angry because he was not what you wished him to be," Dunston said, "because he did not provide for you what you expected of him."

A charge of rage shot through Buceph. "He was a stupid, frightened man, afraid of change, afraid to risk, afraid of life itself. I was not duped by him as you and the others were. Any fool could see that there was much to be done that he did not do."

"Perhaps we who are not fools could not see this so clearly," replied Dunston with a tone of admonishing sarcasm.

Buceph could not contain a brief chuckle which broke the tension a bit, but then he grew wistful and reflective. "When I was young, I looked up to my father, thinking that he was special, believing that he was chosen to make the land prosperous and happy. I was taught of his goodness, kindness and openness. He was highly regarded and I was proud to be his son."

"And how did that change after you came to know him?" Beth asked.

"My Time of Reason was spent watching a pitiful little man sit in his self-pity, unable to decide, unwilling to act, unable to achieve," replied Buceph angrily. "Seeing what my mind did not want to believe, my regard for him turned to sickening disgust as I watched his dreams and mine melt into a pool of apathy."

"Nothing can be gained through time wasted in anger and blame," Beth said.

"I must find the courage to overcome the fear of my father," Buceph stated with firm conviction. "I must *do* what my father *did not,* for I have no intention of being cast in his shadow."

"Then what *are* we to do, Buceph?" Dunston asked.

"My father gave me this crystal," Buceph said, holding it out in his palm. "His dying request was that I use it to summon the Guide and visit the Ascetic."

"And are you going to do it?" Beth asked.

"I suppose I must," Buceph said.

Early the next morning, Buceph journeyed to the Promontory Point alone. He raised the crystal high in the air and he waited. To his surprise, no more than five minutes passed before the Guide appeared beside them. "Are you the Guide of whom my father spoke?" Buceph asked.

"I am," replied the Guide. "I have come so that your father's dying wish might be fulfilled."

"My father told me you would come, though I was hoping you were nothing more than a figment of a demented imagination," Buceph snapped.

"It does not matter whether I am flesh or illusion," the Guide replied, "for *you* see both the same."

"I know that I am to follow you," Buceph said indignantly, "but I fail to see how some old man who has never met me can have any solutions to my problems. I do not need him to lay my duty before me. It has already been done. I already know the direction I must take."

"Then will you follow or will you stay?"

Buceph paused. "Very well," he said at length. "I shall follow, for I shall not let my pride stand before my honor. I shall honor my father's dying wish."

By the time Buceph had risen to his feet, the Guide had disappeared from the spot where he was standing. Looking about anxiously, Buceph spotted him standing at the edge of the forest beckoning with his staff. He set out to catch up to him, but the Guide stayed just ahead and Buceph struggled to keep him in sight through the thick greenery. Up and up he chased the Guide, until the air grew cool and his breath short. Finally, Buceph was delivered to the Ascetic's cave and he approached the old man, panting.

"Please, rest," the Ascetic welcomed. "You look weary."

Buceph leaned against a stump as he caught his breath, then set straight into his introduction. "I am Buceph, son of Aleph and Anna, inheritor of the Prophecy of the Keeper of the Trees. I have entered my Time of Wisdom and I am in your presence at my father's sanction and by his dying request."

"Greetings to you, Buceph. Won't you sit?" the Ascetic said graciously as he pointed his crooked finger toward the stump. "Refresh yourself."

Buceph sat and took a cup of hot tea from the Ascetic's gnarled hands. He blew on the tea to cool it, then took a tentative sip as he looked into the Ascetic's face. "Well?" he said. "You sent for me, so what have you to offer me?"

The Ascetic sat quietly casting his gaze into the fire, saying nothing.

"Old man!" Buceph said impatiently. "We both know what I must do. If there is anything you have to offer me to make my task easier, if there is something I must learn from you, then teach me, else I shall consider my obligation fulfilled."

"Then consider your obligation fulfilled," replied the Ascetic, "for I have nothing to teach you. I am not your advisor but your observer. But if you wish to learn, you are welcome to stay."

Curiosity held Buceph to his spot. He studied the old man for a moment then continued. "According to your Prophecy, this land was chosen to become a haven for Outlanders, a haven for the lost, and I intend to see that it is restored to its intended purpose."

"And just how do you see its purpose, Buceph?"

"I was taught that Oxymora is to be a land of welcome, of freedom, of opportunity, a place where Outlanders might find a home. It is my legacy to see that it serves its purpose well. It is something I believe in."

"Those are noble aspirations, Buceph."

"It is my passion, and I am willing to give my very life to it," Buceph replied. "I know my purpose, and I know my means."

"I am glad that changing the world is left to the young," the Ascetic said with a sigh. "It is only the young who still know everything."

"I shall drive the Malthusians from our land, and even as they flee I shall exact from them full measure of justice to avenge what they have done here."

"Punishment given for abuse received? Pain inflicted for hurt endured? A life taken for a life lost? And after you accomplish this, what will you build from a land which is shamed, hurt and strewn with dead?"

"I grow impatient, old man," said Buceph indignantly, "for it is *your* Prophecy I am destined to fulfill. Why do you make it difficult for me by playing with riddles? Is it not true that success can only follow a victory? And if your words are true, then is it not clear that my duty lies in defeating the Malthusians? Is that not The Way?"

"It is The Way of foolish men to try to conquer that which they cannot abide and wise men to abide that which they cannot conquer. It is foolish men who change the world."

"I am weary of your retorts," Buceph said haughtily. "I need to get on with my work. If you have something of value to me, then I shall listen; else I shall go."

"I acknowledge your anger, and you have a right to it if you choose," conceded the Ascetic, "but your aim is poor, for it is hitting me, and it is not I with whom you are angry. Just what is the object of your anger, Buceph?"

Buceph stared into the old man's kindly eyes. "You are right, Ascetic," he said, realizing that this old man had done nothing to deserve his ire. "I am not angry with you. Forgive me. I do not know why I direct my irritation at you."

"Then what are the causes of your anger, Buceph?"

"I am angry at the injustices, prejudice and inequities my father permitted. I am angry at the Malthusians who have taken what rightfully belongs to Oxymora. I am angry at the loss of those dear to me."

"These are the *objects* of your anger, but they are not its cause," the Ascetic said.

"Then perhaps I am angry because I am lost."

"You are lost because you are angry," replied the Ascetic.

"Very well," Buceph said, "let us stop the riddle. Tell me the cause of my anger."

"Your anger is your fear made visible. It is in your fear that your danger lies--beware it."

Buceph cocked his head to the left and looked inquisitively at the Ascetic. "My father told me that fear was my legacy. He taught me that the only way I could overcome it was to follow The Way." Then, looking back at the fire he added, "But my father was a fool."

"Is that how you see him, Buceph?"

"My father was afraid of everything. He feared drought when the rivers flowed full, he feared famine when the storehouses overflowed, he feared storms on sunny days. To follow The Way as my father did would be to treat my beloved land as he treated it, or worse. I suppose that my greatest fear is being like my father."

"In being afraid of being like your father, you already are," replied the Ascetic. "What do you plan to do differently?"

"I shall not let my fear rule me. My anger shall rule my fear."

"Your fear wears a mask of courage," replied the Ascetic, "but the more bravely you speak, the more your fear shows through."

"I shall never admit to my fear," Buceph said, "To show fear is to show weakness and I shall not be weak like my father. If I am to have brave followers, I must be strong and decisive. If they doubt their leader, they will doubt their mission."

"Then perhaps you *should* have your moment of bravery," the Ascetic said. "You have the rest of your life to be a coward."

Buceph sat thoughtfully for a moment staring at the fire. "There *are* times that I doubt my courage, Ascetic."

"It takes courage to doubt. It is not facing others that we fear, but rather ourselves. Once self is conquered, you will be able to face anything in the world."

"Then I shall lose my fear and when I have the courage, I shall begin my conquest."

"You shall begin your conquest, and when you have the courage, you shall lose your fear. It is then that you will know that the power to force others to yield unto you is not nearly so important as the courage to yield unto yourself."

Buceph said no more. The Ascetic's last point had been a telling one. He wanted to run, he wanted to lash out; he wanted to die. The appearance of the Guide was a welcome relief--he would have to hear no more.

Chapter 15

Retaliation

Buceph returned more subdued than his companions had ever seen him. He was withdrawn and moody, and he said nothing of his visit to the Ascetic. They all knew that the time was at hand when Buceph must take charge of the future of Oxymora. Things would be different now that Buceph was the leader of their nation, but none of them was quite sure how to articulate their changing roles.

It was certain the Malthusian issue would have to be addressed and the task of addressing it would ultimately befall Buceph.

It was equally certain that if this land were to prosper, Buceph must find a way to free it from its bondage, heal the strained relations and ensure prosperity. It would be a monumental task indeed.

It was a month after Buceph's return when Dunston finally approached him. "Do you not think that it is time for us to make plans for our future?" he asked.

"Sometimes one must back away from a problem in order to see it clearly," Buceph replied, avoiding Dunston's question.

"You have not yet spoken of your visit to the Ascetic," Dunston persisted. "What direction did he give you?"

"The Ascetic speaks in riddles," Buceph replied. "It is as if he knows every detail of my destiny, but reveals only portions to me. Listening to him is like trying to solve some cosmic puzzle with some of the pieces missing."

"But what about the Prophecy? What about your legacy? What is to be the fate of our land?" Dunston insisted. "We are sitting here doing nothing while five-hundred Malthusian soldiers slither through the veins of our land.

That is one soldier for every four of our people. They lord over us on every corner of every street in every village. Their spears and knives are always ready to kill anyone who refuses their requests, and occasionally they kill someone just for sport."

Buceph looked Dunston straight in the eye and raised his hand, palm out. "You do not need to remind me of my duty," he said sternly. "The Ascetic told me what my father told me with his dying words--that success can only follow a victory. It is clear enough to everyone that I have been charged with the duty of driving them out."

"Then why are we not about our business?" Dunston asked pointedly.

"The time is not yet right," Buceph replied. "The Malthusians are still on their guard, but in time they will relax their vigil. All lions must sleep. We shall winter here at the Elysian Wood and devise our strategy. Then, with the coming of spring, we shall move upon our enemy."

Dunston softened his approach. "It is an awesome responsibility which has befallen you, Buceph. It is a noble cause and must be pursued with honor. I only fear that our sacrifices will be many."

"Sacrifice is an essential part of achieving anything worthwhile," Buceph replied, "Remember, Dunston, it is only to the best and the strongest that the greatest trials are given."

Dunston said no more. During the ensuing months, he and Buceph considered every possible means of overtaking Malthusian strongholds. Into the winter, they were still mapping their course, discussing strategies, and gathering their courage. They were about to set events into motion which would change their lives forever--events which would usher in the loss of innocence.

Another important event happened that winter--Buceph and Beth became lovers. Though Dunston loved them both deeply and wished to see them happy, he harbored feelings he could neither understand nor explain--jealousy, abandonment, loneliness. He resented their changing roles and, though he kept these things in his heart, a gap developed between them which would never be completely bridged again.

By midwinter Beth was often tearful. The time for their departure was drawing near and she made her dissatisfaction known. Her vigil at the Elysian Wood would be filled with loneliness and worry.

It was late winter when Buceph somberly announced that the time had come to begin their conquest. Beth burst into tears. "Please don't do this thing."

"Don't be afraid, Beth," Buceph said soothingly. "We have planned well. We will not be harmed."

"Why do you persist in the notion that you can fight them?" Beth asked through angry tears. "You know you have not the weapons nor the army to engage the Malthusians. You know they will kill you!"

"Buceph is right, Beth" Dunston chimed in. "The Malthusians are many and their weapons superior, but they fight noisily in the open. They do not know how to fight without their disciplined order, and especially not in darkness. We will camp in the forests by day, then by the dark of night we shall creep into their strongholds like a slow fog. They will never know what struck them and they cannot hurt what they cannot see."

"But who will you find to join your band?" Beth asked. "Who will be foolish enough to risk their lives to follow you?"

"The Hedons," Buceph replied. "It is the Year of the Star and it is already half the size of the moon. Its coming will instill terror in most, but life on the edge will only seem a little sweeter to the Hedons. They are the ones who will fling caution to the wind, believing that they will probably die anyway. When we offer to pay them for devilish deeds they would gladly do for free, they will follow us to hell if we ask."

"And how do you plan to pay them?" Beth asked.

"I have my inheritance," Buceph replied. "We will offer them decent wages and promise them the spoils from their attacks. Malthusian weapons are much coveted and bring high prices."

"But I have had a dream, Buceph," Beth protested in a final desperate plea.

"Then tell us," Buceph said somewhat condescendingly.

"A knight was pursuing a giant serpent who terrorized the land, but each time the knight struck the serpent with his sword, the serpent would swish its tail wiping out crops and forests. Then it would spew fire from its mouth, burning homes and villages and it would stomp its gigantic feet, crushing fleeing people in its path. The harder the knight fought, the more enraged the beast became, and it unleashed its fury on everyone the knight knew and loved. But the Knight was determined to slay the serpent and he continued to fight."

Beth began to cry once more. Buceph placed his arms lovingly around her. "And how did your dream end?" he asked gently.

Beth pulled away from him, burying her face in her hands. "The people finally took up their arms and slew the knight they loved so they could live in peace with the serpent they despised."

Buceph hung his head, turned and walked away.

Trada was not at all what Buceph and Dunston had expected. Storehouses had been rebuilt, homes were under construction, the marketplace had been resurrected and business was taking place as usual. The Malthusians had rebuilt Trada to serve Malthusian needs and they were governing it with martial law.

Avoiding the watchful eye of the Malthusians, the pair began gathering their bandit band. They lived with the Hedons in sordid back rooms, in alleys, on the docks, and little by little they picked the most able, the most ruthless, the most greedy.

When they numbered thirty, they set out for the Dark Forest. The Hedons were reluctant at first, but when Buceph assured them that Aleph had spent a year there alone and could not be found, they figured it would be a safe place to retreat to after their raids.

There, Dunston and Buceph armed their band of rebels as best they could, though they had but slings and bows made for hunting.

Though swiftly picked and poorly trained, within a month they had shaped this misguided concoction of humanity into an adequate fighting force capable of executing effective sneak attacks.

With the coming of spring, they engaged their first objective--the tiny village of Ferme in the fertile valley along the river. Ferme was the distribution center for the army's food supply and disrupting their distribution of food would create confusion and distract their attentions.

Under the cloak of darkness they encircled the village. There were soldiers posted all over town in groups of three and four, a hundred paces apart. A quick assessment told Aleph that his small group was outnumbered by at least three to one. The soldiers were around small campfires, some laughing, some gambling, some napping, all off-guard.

Buceph's rebels silently poised themselves with bows, systematically aiming their arrows at thirty soldiers. When Aleph gave the word, twenty-seven Malthusians dropped with the first sally.

In confusion and fear, the remaining soldiers scrambled to form defensive ranks. Almost instinctively, the Malthusians scrambled to the center of the village, formed a protective circle, and made an umbrella with their shields. The outer circle of soldiers drew their swords for close fighting, while the inner group drew spears for distance, but there was no one to fight. Malthusian military tactics may have worked well in the light of day on the battlefield, but this posture gave them no advantage in the dark against an enemy they could not see.

While a second wave of arrows rained down upon the soldiers, Aleph, Dunston and two others chosen from their band set fire to a hay wagon and sent it rolling downhill toward the tightly grouped ranks. Not only did the blazing projectile get the attention of the Malthusians, it broke their ranks and sent them scurrying to safety.

The third wave came in the form of fifteen arrows and fifteen sharp stones hurled from slings, and twenty-two more soldiers either died or were wounded sufficiently to be rendered helpless or harmless.

With only about forty soldiers remaining and all their leadership dead, the Malthusians lost all semblance of an organized force. They scattered, running from their unseen enemy, hiding in doorways, under baskets, in tiny nooks and crevices, anywhere a dark corner offered a place to conceal themselves.

Buceph's band, now armed with Malthusian swords and spears, formed an impenetrable wall of men and weapons, the full thirty strong. House by house, building by building, alley by alley, they flushed out each soldier, one by one, until they had slaughtered the last one. Then silently, swiftly, they disappeared back into the darkness of the forest to hide from the light of day.

Dunston was sickened by the slaughter. The reality of slitting the throat or bashing the skull of another human being was almost more than he could bear. Buceph on the other hand exuded a coolness, a satisfaction, as if a hunger had just been fed. Letting out his rage on the Malthusians had relaxed him and brought him a strange and comforting peace and he thirsted for more.

It was a scant two weeks after their first attack when they launched their second. This target was larger, more dangerous--the village of Copperton which lay to the southwest in the foothills of the Copper Mountains. Here the Malthusians had taken control of the mining and transporting of the copper.

The diversion they had created in Ferme, the element of surprise, and their shield of darkness gave the rebel band a tactical edge once more. Their slings and arrows were now supplemented by the finest Malthusian weapons, but their real advantage came in the unorthodox approach they took to battle. The Malthusian army, fighting by military rules, offered little resistance to the sneaky, stealthy, night-cloaked maneuvers the rebel band employed. Though there were more than a hundred soldiers defending this village, the rebel band found it an easy victory.

Buceph's eyes gleamed with pleasure as he lashed out at the Malthusians, and even Dunston found the killing a little easier to justify; the guilt a little easier to ignore.

By the time the news of Buceph's attacks reached Malthusian military headquarters in Trada, the rebels had already mounted attacks on a half dozen other occupied villages. They overthrew villages with practiced ease, and caused substantial disruption to Malthusian military order.

Tales of Buceph's exploits spread quickly, and his surly band soon became heroes to the Oxymoran people. Their countrymen supported their efforts completely, carefully guarding their whereabouts, providing them with food and shelter, offering to help in any way.

By midsummer, they were preparing to attack the military headquarters at Trada. They were seasoned now; ready to take on the Elite Guard. Like an invisible fog, they eased softly into Trada just past midnight--ten from the east, ten from the north, ten from the south. In pairs, they attacked the lone soldiers who were posted on the edge of town and silently cut their throats.

Around the marketplace and the docks, the rebels caught small groups of soldiers off their guard or sleeping. Two or three complacent soldiers provided almost no resistance to the ten guerillas attacking them, and within the first quarter hour, Buceph's band had swiftly, surely and silently disposed of more than fifty soldiers.

They regrouped at the town square and headed for the Malthusian's camp which housed another fifty sleeping Malthusian Guard. The city of tents was near the warehouses which lined the docks. Slithering between the buildings, Buceph's band took their positions, surrounding the camp. When Buceph gave the signal, his men began setting fire to the tents, and as the sleep-grogged soldiers ran for safety, Buceph's men slaughtered them with swords, knives, spears, and clubs.

With Anna's Cove to their backs, the Malthusians had no route of escape, and few of them had time to don their armor and weapons. No more than a half-hour had passed, and the entire Malthusian contingent in Trada had been slaughtered. Little by little, Buceph's band was chipping away at Malthusian rule, and this had been their most important victory.

Chapter 16

An Admission of Defeat

By the end of the month, Buceph's little band had substantially beaten the Malthusians. Though some two-hundred Malthusian soldiers remained, they had seen enough and lost enough, and they boarded their ships and fled back to Malthus.

From the tales the soldiers told, it appeared to Vistar that all of Oxymora had taken up arms, and even the soldiers would never have believed that there were only thirty.

"Bring me my generals!" Vistar screamed at the top of his lungs, and they were in his presence within minutes. "I want Buceph and I want him now! Take what you need to take, do what you need to do, kill who you need to kill, but get him! And I want him alive! I will be there by the third moon, and I fully expect him to be jailed when I arrive."

Vistar's generals promptly dispatched two-thousand of the finest Malthusian Guard, twice Oxymora's population, to put a stop to the rebellion. By the following month, a battalion of heavily armed Malthusians arrived on Oxymoran shores.

Though Buceph and his band had won a decisive battle over the initial Malthusian presence, Buceph's dream now began to crumble. Malthusians were ever-present now; watching, guarding, restraining, interrogating. Their sheer numbers were overwhelming, and they had learned to remain on their guard day and night.

Life for the Oxymoran people became a prison. Freedoms were stripped, they could no longer assemble, move or speak freely, and they could no longer find ways to support Buceph's band with food and lodging.

This only inflamed Buceph's anger and he defiantly intensified the savagery of his attacks, raiding Malthusian camps from dusk to dawn. He was taking more risks than ever before and, for the first time, members of his band were being killed. He lost four men in three raids.

Dunston and the men protested their escalating losses, but Buceph stubbornly maintained that their persistent antagonism would eventually produce enough discouragement to drive the Malthusians out for good.

Unfortunately, the Malthusians had also escalated their retaliations. Intent on suppressing the uprising, they searched the forests for the outlaws, killing innocent people and burning homes. By the end of summer, two Oxymorans had been slaughtered for every Malthusian lost. A full third of the population of Oxymora had been wiped out.

By fall, the rebels were forced to take respite from their onslaught. The Star was beginning to pierce their cloak of darkness, for it was now half the size of the moon, and they retreated into the Dark Forest to bind their wounds and rest their spirits.

As Buceph and Dunston sat exhausted by the campfire wondering what their next move was to be, Dunston spoke. "There is unrest among the ranks. They have seen too much blood for too little reward and the Star is making them irritable and restless."

Buceph did not reply.

"Do you remember Beth's dream about the knight and the serpent, Buceph?" Dunston asked. "It has come to pass. We have unleashed the serpent's wrath upon our people. Our band is weary and the Star has brought hopelessness with it once more."

"Are the people wavering in their support of our cause as well?" Buceph asked.

"No," Dunston replied, "they remain loyal to a fault, but I fear that they will not survive our nobility."

"You know the Ascetic's words as well as I, Dunston," Buceph said. "Success can only follow a victory."

"I have no reason to doubt them, for I heard your father speak those words with his dying breath."

"All I do is for the fulfillment of that end."

"I was not questioning your intentions, but rather our actions," Dunston replied. "Our attacks on the Malthusians are causing severe retaliation. Far too many are suffering and dying to further our cause."

"People die in war," Buceph said coldly. "Have you forgotten that your mother and mine were victims of Malthusian cruelty?"

"I have not forgotten," Dunston replied, "but if revenge is our only motive, then my loyalty has been to foolishness. Can you not see that our people are paying too high a price for your revenge?"

"Our people are paying for my father's mistakes, not for my revenge," Buceph snapped. "It was my father who delivered our people into Malthusian hands. It is *his* failure that has killed them."

"The fault was not your father's," Dunston said, trying to reason with Buceph. "He followed The Way as best he knew, and he fathered a haven for the lost, just as the Prophecy foretold."

"If you cannot see what he was, then you are a boundless fool as well," Buceph snapped.

Dunston was taken aback. "So *that* is how you are able to be cruel to others without guilt," he said in dismay. "You blame it all on your father!"

Buceph's face grew red, for his companion's words rang of truth denied. "I blame it on him because that is where the responsibility lies!"

Dunston shook his head. "You will never learn from your mistakes as long as you deny you have made any."

"And you sound just like him!" Buceph said. "If you are to live in his cowardly shadow and by his cowardly ways, then I have no more use for your aid than for his legacy."

Buceph's words stung Dunston deeply. "I can no longer reason with you, Buceph," he said. "Reason has limits, but your rage knows no bounds."

Turning his back to Dunston, Buceph replied arrogantly, "I give you audience only that I might use your ideas, but I shall entrust power to you no longer, lest we be defeated by your stupidity. Your opinion is worth to me what I have given for it--absolutely nothing. And do not forget your place, for you are but a lowly servant, while I am born of prophecy."

Dunston's chin dropped, his eyes widened in disbelief, his face drew firm, as he squared his shoulders and peered straight ahead, eyes fixed on some distant point. "Yes, my master, I shall obey," he replied with cold, sarcastic bitterness.

Looking into his brother's eyes, Buceph knew that he had overstepped his bounds. "Dunston, I didn't. . . ."

"I no longer know you, Buceph," Dunston interrupted. "You have become a dark creature so filled with self that you cannot separate rage from reality. I have already gone too far just to keep your stubborn pride afloat, for you have held on to it long after you had nothing left to be proud of." With that, Dunston turned his back on Buceph and tucked himself into his bedroll.

Alone that night in his bed, Buceph faced the truth that Dunston had spoken. His sleep was restless and disturbed, his dreams filled with knights and serpents. An owl's shrill screech jarred him awake and he bolted upright, shivering and sweating. He felt trapped--no way to fight and nowhere to run. His plan unraveled, Buceph had hit a wall of confusion. Devastated by his failure, he had lost the faith he once had in himself, and he knew that without Dunston he could achieve nothing.

With the dawn, Buceph awoke to find Dunston gone. He jumped to his feet and called to him, hoping to find him and set right the damage he had done. As he looked around the camp, his heart sank as he realized that his rebel band had deserted during the night. Not one of them remained. Buceph stood for a long time, empty and angry that his plans had failed.

A thin stream of smoke rose above the bank of the river, and Buceph went to investigate. There, Dunston had built a fire and was sitting pensively with a cup of hot tea, poking the glowing coals with a stick. Buceph approached quietly, wishing to choose his words carefully in order to regain his companion's confidence.

"Their loyalty was only to their own greed and pleasures," Dunston said without turning.

Buceph walked to the other side of the fire, poured a cup of hot tea, and sat, never taking his eyes from his companion's face. "You have been hurt by my words, and though you may no longer feel loyalty to me, I must know if you remain loyal to our cause. If we fight amongst ourselves, someone else will surely win."

"I shall allow neither your arrogance nor my own pride to stand before reason," Dunston said, looking Buceph in the eye, "and I believed that you would not either. Now I see that it is futile to try to reason the stubbornness out of you, for it was not reasoned into you." Dunston returned his somber gaze back to the fire. "My allegiance shall no longer belong to you. It shall be given only to higher purposes."

Buceph stood and walked around the fire toward Dunston, then he stood directly over him and look down into his face. "Does that mean that you will continue to follow me, Dunston, or will you go your own way?"

"My loyalty is to our homeland," Dunston replied with eyes locked directly on Buceph's. "If I must follow you to be true to that loyalty, then I shall follow you. If I must attack you to be true to that loyalty, then I shall attack you."

It was clear that the friendship and trust Buceph had valued for so many years had been destroyed. "There is nothing left here for us to do here," Buceph said. "It is time to go home."

Both were silent as they began their journey--Dunston nursing his wounds, and Buceph wallowing in remorse over his attack on his good friend. At dusk, they camped on the western slope of the great mountain near the edge of the Dark Forest. As they sat quietly by the camp fire, Buceph took the crystal from around his neck and held it tightly. "I must visit the Ascetic," he said. "You go ahead of me and tell Beth that I will be home in a couple of days." With that, Buceph left his companion and set out for the Promontory Point, crystal in hand.

Buceph's journey to the Ascetic was long and arduous with the added weight of defeat heavy upon him. He was filled with dread at having to admit his failure, for to do so would be to admit he was like his father.

The Ascetic was gracious as usual, inviting Buceph to sit and share his cup. "Well, Buceph," the Ascetic began, "you look battle-weary."

"I am, Ascetic," Buceph replied. "We have been fighting the Malthusians, trying to drive them from our land."

"When you believe that something should be so, it is natural to put energy into trying to make it so."

"And we did make it so," Buceph said. "We succeeded in driving them from our homeland, but they have returned with greater force than ever and their retaliations on innocent Oxymoran people have been devastating."

"Attacking the problem usually has a way of making the problem worse," the Ascetic said. "It is easy to mistake activity for accomplishment."

"But how can we have the victory spoken in the Prophecy if we do not attack the problem?"

"One can accomplish by surrender what cannot be done by force," the Ascetic replied. "Victory can only be avoided by focusing one's energies on the problem instead of surrendering to a solution. When you surrender to a solution, the problem will go away."

"Then what *is* the solution, Ascetic?"

"The only way to conquer an enemy is to become a friend."

Buceph laughed aloud. "I am hardly in a position to befriend the Malthusians. There is too much anger between us."

"But it is *your* anger that separates you."

Buceph's face grew serious. "If I did surrender, it would stop much pain and suffering, but such a radical move seems unreasonable."

"And which are you, Buceph, a reasonable man or an unreasonable man?"

Buceph paused reflectively, transfixed by the fire. "Dunston says that I am an unreasonable man. He says that my anger makes me so."

"And is Dunston a reasonable man?"

"He is the most reasonable man I have met," Buceph replied, "and he is right. I am an unreasonable man and I reacted to my anger instead of responding to his needs."

"It is no more possible to force a reasonable man to see things from an unreasonable point of view that to force an unreasonable man to see things from a reasonable point of view," the Ascetic said. "But it is unreasonable men who force the world to change while reasonable men spend their lives adapting to its changes."

"I know now that trying to make Dunston see things my way was a mistake, but that is not where it ended. When he would not see things my way, I exercised my authority over him and hurt him deeply. I am not so sure that I am so sure any longer."

"When you are sure of The Way, it becomes unimportant to persuade others to follow," the Ascetic said.

"But I was not sure of The Way, and when I could not persuade him to see things my way, I loosed sharp words which cannot be retrieved and our bitter exchange has haunted me since."

"The Way of understanding prevents many regrets in moments of anger," the Ascetic said. "Harming Dunston was not born of malice, but of lack of understanding."

"But I thought I understood him and he understood me. I took for granted that he shared my views and that he would follow me always."

"Perhaps he believed he walked beside you," replied the Ascetic.

The Keeper of the Trees

Buceph's face flushed, his ears rang, his vision blurred. Truth had finally pierced his wall of defense. "I now understand what you meant when you told me that in my anger, my danger lies. It has the power to make enemies of friends and friends of enemies. It has been my greatest source of strength and my greatest weakness. It has rallied people about me and pushed people away. It has given me power and revealed my vulnerabilities. It has spurred me to conquer and it has conquered me. Why could you not have shown me The Way?"

"The Way is before you always, but it is not illuminated by advice," the Ascetic replied. "It is only revealed through experience."

"But must I experience defeat to gain my victory?"

"It is in defeat that character is built; in victory, the serpent is revealed."

Buceph was taken aback. "You know of Beth's dream?"

"I know of truth, and truth lies in dreams," the Ascetic replied, "but even truth comes and goes."

"What do you mean, Ascetic?" Buceph asked. "Truth is truth."

"Truth changes, Buceph," the Ascetic replied. "Truth says that man cannot fly, but wisdom says flight is possible. When man does learn to fly, the truth will change, but not the wisdom."

"Then what wisdom am I to gain from defeat?"

"In order to truly understand flight, one must fly. In order to truly understand the serpent, one must become the serpent."

"But I do not wish to become the serpent, for the serpent is but an author of evil."

"Do not worry, Buceph, for it is not you who will be deemed worthy to live as a serpent."

"Worthy!" Buceph snapped. "What worthiness could lie in becoming a serpent?"

"All things have their purpose, and the purpose of one is no higher or lower than the purpose of any other."

Buceph gazed up at the sky. "Then what is the purpose of the Star?" Buceph asked pensively.

"It is both a messenger of destruction and a promise of hope," the Ascetic replied. "There can be no new without old, no beginnings without endings, no building without tearing down."

"And a new world cannot be born without suffering the loss of the old one?" Buceph asked.

"That is The Way of things," the Ascetic replied. "Nothing can be created unless something else is destroyed. Animals are destroyed that we might have food, people are destroyed that we might have peace, trees are destroyed that we might have homes."

Buceph was quiet for a time. New understanding shown from his face. "But new trees will grow," he said.

"You are learning again, Buceph," the Ascetic acknowledged, as he nodded toward the Guide. Buceph's visit had come to an end.

Chapter 17

A Time to Surrender

The Star was cresting as Buceph made his way toward the Elysian Wood. It had come so close this time, half the size of the moon, and it spewed a brilliant tail which stretched across half the sky. Buceph found himself both relieved and strangely disappointed when it began to wane--another twenty years lay ahead and he was not sure he wanted to face them. He was even less certain that he wished to be around for the next coming of the Star. Even if it didn't strike, it would pass so close that it would surely cause destruction and chaos.

Their cave was a welcome sight indeed. As he approached, he caught sight of a figure in the distance. It was Dunston, and he was running, screaming at the top of his lungs, "It's a boy! You have a son! He came with the passing of the Star!"

Buceph was speechless. He had not a hint, not a clue. His thoughts, his feelings, his very soul had been so occupied by the Malthusians that the idea of becoming a father had never occurred to him.

He entered the cave, almost reverently, and crept silently over to Beth. She was sleeping. He stood there admiring her beauty and an intense feeling of love welled up from deep inside him. It was a feeling he had not experienced in quite some time.

Then his eyes widened as he gazed in wonder across the room to the tiny blanketed basket which held his son. In that instant, his mind turned completely from fighting and killing to the new hope which lay there sleeping so innocently.

Beth aroused from her slumber and smiled warmly when she saw Buceph gazing at his son. Buceph jumped with a start when she took his hand. "He is the one, Buceph," she said. "He is the Keeper of the Trees."

"How do you know this, Beth?"

"I do not know how I know, Buceph. I just know," she said, and Buceph took her knowing deep into his heart.

A month passed. It was evening, and the Star was still waning above the southern horizon. Beth, Buceph and Dunston were sitting by the fire, and Dunston was fidgeting in his chair. "Buceph," he began, "I must tell you what is happening in Trada. The Malthusians are searching for us. I shudder to think what will happen to us when we are captured, but I am more concerned over the fate of Beth and your son. Each of our men in turn has been arrested and questioned, then set free in return for telling all they knew. Unfortunately, our brave and loyal followers have been exceedingly cooperative with the Malthusians. Many of them have joined in the search in hopes of collecting the bounty for our capture." He paused. "Buceph, I need not tell you what they might do to Beth and Kimrey if they find us here. What are we to do?"

"I must surrender. I am the one Vistar really wants," Buceph said without hesitation.

Beth's eyes widened, her jaw dropped. "You know that if you do, Vistar will likely take great pleasure in your torture and death."

"Then so be it," Buceph replied staunchly. "You know as well as I that we cannot continue to fight, and where would we flee? The only honorable thing to do is to surrender. It is The Way."

"That is very noble indeed," Dunston said. "And what do you expect that will achieve?"

"The Ascetic has shown me that a direct attack is least effective and that surrender can achieve what force cannot. The Way for me is to surrender."

"And what makes you believe that his guidance will work better this time than it did the last?" Beth asked.

Buceph stared at the floor. "I was not truthful with either of you. It was not the Ascetic who guided me to attack the Malthusians. It was my anger. I obeyed my rage over my reason."

"I thought as much!" Beth replied, standing and putting her hands on her hips. "How dare you manipulate us with lies! What gives you the right to jeopardize our safety? Who do you think you are, that you can make decisions affecting my life without consulting me? Do you have any idea what it was like for me while you were gone? Do you care?" With that, she burst into tears, turned on her heels and left the room.

Buceph was shocked at Beth's outburst. "What is eating her?" he asked, turning to Dunston.

"She is right, you know," Dunston replied, "but it is too late to start worrying about anyone's feelings now, even if you were capable of doing so. The only thing that matters is finding a way out of our current dilemma."

Buceph shook his head and stared at the floor. "I have always tried to do what I thought best for everyone."

"Unfortunately, you do not have the wisdom to judge that nor the power to control it," Dunston replied.

"My surrender is our only course," Buceph insisted, looking Dunston squarely in the eye.

Dunston studied Buceph for a moment. "It is clear that you are willing to set yourself aside for the greater good, Buceph, but I do not yet see what purpose it will serve. What makes you think your surrender will solve anything?"

"It is our sword, Dunston. It is the way we shall defeat the enemy."

Dunston's shoulders slumped. He shook his head and stared blankly at Buceph. "You have not lost your obsession at all! Just when I thought you had succumbed to nobility, you are planning a new attack!"

"If I lose my obsession, Dunston, I may be losing the best part of me," Buceph said with a grin.

Dunston could not help but chuckle, but he quickly grew serious again. "But how will your surrender defeat the Malthusians?" he asked, dumbfounded.

"It has been more than two years since Malthus lost their trade with Carpathia. I am willing to gamble that they are suffering deeply without the motherland and, if that is true, the only way Vistar can mend relations is to free Oxymora and restore peace and harmony. If he is to do that, he needs me. If he needs me, I have the advantage. If he does not kill me, then he must surrender to me."

"All right, I can see how that might help to free our land, but I still do not see how your surrender will bring the victory you so eagerly pursue."

"I assumed that it would be obvious to you, Dunston. You follow The Way! Does it not say that there is strength in weakness, victory in surrender? Is it not the victim who ultimately emerges victorious? Do you not see? *We* are the oppressed, *we* are the downtrodden, *we* are the injured party. If Vistar is to regain favor with Carpathia, he must be diligent in his efforts to see that we are well-compensated, well-protected and well-cared-for. He will, in effect, become our servant."

Dunston bit his lip nervously, then continued. "And what if you are wrong, and Vistar puts you to death?"

"I have thought this over carefully, Dunston. Vistar is a brutal ruler, but I do not believe that he is so blinded by arrogance that he would further jeopardize his country's relations with Carpathia just to satisfy his urge for revenge. He knows that killing the monarch of a recognized government would be taken quite seriously by the Carpathians. He knows that they might go beyond refusing trade and declare war."

Dunston stared blankly into Buceph's eyes for a long moment, then shook his head and smiled. "I have never understood you, Buceph, but I suppose it is the right thing to do even if it is for the wrong reasons. What is it you wish me to do?"

"Seek out Oberon. He hopes as much as anyone that the occupation of Oxymora will cease and that trade will return to normal. Have him take a message to the Malthusian Magistrate in Trada offering my surrender in return for your freedom and the reward they are offering. The reward for my capture will provide for Beth and Kimrey for a time."

"Very well," Dunston replied. "I will do your bidding."

Buceph looked Dunston straight in the eye and grasped him by the shoulders. "You must assure me that you will care for Beth and Kimrey."

"Of course I will care for them," Dunston replied, pulling away from Buceph's grasp.

Buceph smiled wistfully and clasped his hands together. "When you have Oberon's assurance that the Malthusians will accept my surrender on these terms, you can rest assured that my plan will work."

Chapter 18

The Tables Turn

And so it was that Dunston set out for Trada to seek Oberon's help. It was no easy matter moving through the countryside and the streets of the port city without being recognized, but Dunston stealthily made his way to Oberon's estate. There, Oberon welcomed him with open arms and agreed to meet with the Magistrate and negotiate Buceph's surrender. Within a day, he returned with a reply. The Magistrate had guaranteed both the reward and Dunston's pardon in return for Buceph's capture. He had written this on parchment and placed his seal upon it. Buceph was to be delivered to the Malthusians within three days.

The following day, Dunston returned to the Elysian Wood with the news. "Our plan is working, Dunston," Buceph said.

"I do not envy your position, Buceph," Dunston said, "but I know that you must do this thing."

"Go ahead of me and spread the word of my surrender. I want many witnesses to this. It will lend power to our position. I will be there in two days."

And so Dunston set out once more for Trada, but this time he was shouting the news of Buceph's surrender and of a return to peace. Buceph's way was paved with gratitude. As he made his way to Trada the people left their fields and their labors and followed him in support of his bravery.

Dunston met Buceph near Trada and, crowd in tow, they marched boldly through the streets to the town square. Dunston ushered Buceph up to the Magistrate as promised, and Buceph surrendered his sword proudly. The

Magistrate quickly placed Buceph under arrest and paid Dunston his bounty as agreed.

The crowd's cheers turned to jeers as they shackled Buceph's hands and feet, but a hush fell over them as he turned to speak. "Protest not this action, for it is our victory. Rejoice, for our liberation is at hand."

The crowd silently watched the soldiers take him away. They came no nearer understanding Buceph's attitude than did Dunston, but they trusted his words. Buceph was placed in a tiny, makeshift cell in a warehouse near the docks, and a dozen soldiers were posted to guard him day and night.

Dunston returned to the Elysian Wood and set about caring for Beth and Kimrey according to Buceph's wish. It was an uneasy time and they both carried much worry over Buceph's fate though they spoke little of it.

A month passed, and Buceph remained in his cell while the Magistrate awaited Vistar's arrival. When Vistar's ship docked at Trada, a crowd began to gather. The crowd grew as they followed Vistar and his personal guard to the warehouse where Buceph was being held.

Vistar burst into the warehouse, unannounced and without ceremony. "Take me to him!" he demanded, and the Magistrate promptly ushered Vistar to Buceph's tiny cell, soldiers at each flank. "Well, Buceph," he began, "you have caused us a lot of trouble. What do you suppose I should do with you?"

"It is obvious that you do not know, else you would not have come so far to consult me," Buceph said cockily.

Vistar's face flushed, his eyes narrowed, his nostrils flared. "Leave us!" he commanded, and the Magistrate and the guards snapped immediately to his order, closing the cell door behind them. Vistar whirled around to face Buceph. "I can crush you like a grape, you little bastard," he snarled.

"Then why have you not done so, Vistar?" Buceph asked daringly.

Vistar glared at Buceph but did not reply.

"It looks as though we finally have the advantage," Buceph continued boldly. "Are you going to get to the point, or shall we continue to dance?"

Vistar gritted his teeth, but calmed himself quickly. He knew that intimidation would not achieve his end. "Very well, Buceph," he said, humbling himself a bit. "Malthus cannot survive without trade with Carpathia. There are too many things we have grown dependent upon that only Carpathia can provide--foodstuffs and cloth and medicines--and in

107

quantities that Oxymora cannot provide. Anarchy will soon erupt if we do not rekindle our trade with the motherland."

"Then why do you not just conquer Carpathia as well?" Buceph asked sarcastically. "Aggression seems to be your solution to everything."

"You know very well that would be like a dog attacking a tree," admitted Vistar. "There is no power on earth that could conquer the motherland."

Buceph sat back on his cot and folded his arms confidently. "Then just what do you propose, Vistar?"

"I can make you a very wealthy man, Buceph."

"And at what expense is my great wealth to come?"

"All you need do is convince the Carpathian diplomats that Oxymora chooses to become a Malthusian territory. Convince them that it is to your benefit to align your government with ours and that it is your choice to do so. Once our trade with them is reestablished, I will appoint you governor of Oxymora. You will have the power to amass all the riches you desire."

"And then what happens to Oxymora once it comes willingly under your rule?"

"What do you care? You will be rich beyond your grandest dreams."

Buceph brushed the reply aside. "What happens, Vistar?" he insisted leaning forward on his cot. "What happens after I prostitute myself?"

"Buceph! Where is your trust?" Vistar said. "All I am asking is that you restore and abide by your father's agreement with us, giving us the rights to the copper, and we will pay your workers fairly in return. For so long as you keep your father's agreement, Oxymora will live without fear of our imposition. Your land will be restored. You will no longer be under our military rule. All your resources will be returned to you--except the copper, of course."

"My father gave his life to correct that mistake, and as long as I am Monarch of this land, I do not intend to see his mistake repeated," Buceph replied quite assertively.

Vistar's face reddened. His eyes grew dark and scowling. "Then you shall be Monarch over nothing! We shall keep your land and all of its resources! Your people will continue to live in servitude! Since we have nothing more to lose, your suffering shall be our consolation."

"Come now Vistar! I know that the infliction of suffering has brought you much pleasure, but when has it ever brought you any gain?"

Vistar stared menacingly, but calmed himself a bit. "I'm listening, Buceph," he replied, swallowing his pride.

Buceph smiled and began his proposal. "You are a practical man, Vistar, and a stunning mathematician. I'll wager that you would prefer even a small piece of something great over the whole of something worthless. Let me offer you a compromise, my wise adversary."

Vistar paced the cell. "Go on."

"I will help you restore your trade with Carpathia, but only under these three conditions. First, you will completely relinquish control of Oxymora. Second, you will rebuild everything you have destroyed. Third, you will return to us ten of your best tools and ten of your best weapons in payment for each boat load of copper we deliver. When the first two conditions have been met, I can report with integrity to the Carpathian diplomats that we have struck a peace that will be as lasting as the third condition."

Vistar paced angrily to and fro, contemplating Buceph's offer.

"Come now Vistar," Buceph continued, "it is a simple choice. Deal fairly with us or watch your land deteriorate into chaos."

Vistar turned toward the window and stood, tapping his hands together behind his back.

"It is the only way I will cooperate with you, Vistar," Buceph continued. "I will not compromise the dignity of my people for less. You see, we too, have nothing to lose. Nothing in your power can harm us now. You can continue to kill our bodies, destroy our homes, take our resources, but you cannot win, for we shall never give you our allegiance."

Vistar turned and looked Buceph in the eye. "Is that your final word, Buceph?"

"No, Vistar, that is not my final word. If you do not accept my offer, we shall reek such havoc on our own land that you will never take anything of value from it again. *That* is my final word! We value freedom and honor over safety and order, and if this situation cannot be resolved for the good of all, then it shall not be resolved for the good of any."

Vistar thought for a moment, then nodded his head. "Very well then, I shall agree, but do not sleep too soundly, Buceph," he said, turning on his heels. "Come with me."

Buceph slowly rose from his cot and followed cautiously. Emerging from the cell, Vistar and Buceph faced the crowd. A hush fell as Vistar stepped forward. "As of this day, Malthus shall no longer hold claim to this land. I hereby order all Malthusian soldiers to return home. Henceforth, the rule of Oxymora shall be returned to its rightful heir--Buceph."

The crowd stood for a moment in paralyzed silence, and then Oxymorans and Malthusians alike cheered Vistar's proclamation. After all the fighting, all the anger, all the pain, peace had finally come. It was not a perfect peace, but for the moment, Malthus was a most comforting adversary. The crowd entered into raucous celebration, but Buceph wasted no time exercising his new-found freedom. The moment he could break away from the well-wishers, he set out for the Elysian Wood to reunite with Beth and Dunston.

He fairly skipped along, a renewed air of excitement, hope and anticipation coursing through his veins. The Ascetic was right! He had surrendered and he had won!

Chapter 19

A Love Lost

Beth clasped her hands to her face and let out a scream when she spied Buceph on the trail. She was sobbing as she ran to meet him. They rushed together and held one another tightly. "We were sure they had killed you."

Dunston, hearing Beth's cries, dropped his fishing nets and ran up from the river, but stopped short when he saw that it was Buceph. "I see that they have not killed you," he called from the bank.

"You sound disappointed, my old friend," Buceph shouted back. "Vistar has found it more advantageous to cooperate rather than to rule. He has returned the throne to me."

"And what did you exchange for it?" Dunston asked.

Buceph was taken aback by Dunston's skepticism. "I will tell you of our terms in due time, Dunston. It is time to celebrate. We have won our victory as the Ascetic predicted."

Dunston turned and walked back toward the river. Beth's gaze followed him until he disappeared below the bank. "His trust bears scars, Buceph," she said, "as does mine."

"I think that you are both angry that I did not die," Buceph said flatly, "but I can do nothing to change your feelings." He paused, then turned and looked into Beth's face.

"You are right, Buceph. You can do nothing to change my feelings."

"Beth, we are free. Even as we speak, there is a great celebration under way in Trada and messengers have been dispatched throughout the land with the news. We must go to Bonaventure. The war has cost us much and there is much rebuilding to do."

Beth turned her face away and toward the ground. "I cannot go with you, Buceph."

Buceph was stunned. His stomach went queasy. His knees went weak. "What are you saying, Beth? You are everything to me."

"I cannot spend my life waiting and wondering, Buceph. You are married to your position and that is as it should be, but I need more. I need someone who will be there for me and for Kimrey. I need someone I can trust. I need someone who will not try to control my destiny."

"But I will be there, now," Buceph protested. "I will be there to care for you and Kimrey. Don't you understand that I have changed?"

"I know you, Buceph. You will be there until another crisis demands your attention and then you will be gone and I will be left alone with your lies."

"But Beth, why now, just when we have the chance to be together?" Buceph asked with rising fear.

"Perhaps it is our togetherness that puts distance between us, Buceph," Beth replied. "It is only in our separation that we are close. We have failed to grow together and thus we have grown apart."

"It seems that you find no such distance with Dunston," he said, choking back tears of angry frustration. "Is that right, Beth?"

She stroked his cheek with the back of her hand. "I have had to grow strong in your absence and I do not intend to lose what I have gained. Dunston and I intend to raise Kimrey here and to school him in Trada. There he will learn to follow The Way."

There were tears streaming down Buceph's face now. "But there is so much more opportunity for him in Bonaventure," he pleaded, "and I know you would be happy there as well."

"Buceph!" Beth said. "This is the first time in a long while that I have seen you without your wall of pride, but my mind is set. I can no longer permit you to control me with your lies and manipulations. It is a matter of honor to my ideals and kindness to myself."

Buceph sobbed. "I have held on to my stubborn pride long after I had nothing to be proud of. Please come with me," he pleaded pitifully. "Give me a chance to make you happy."

"You do not know me, Buceph," Beth said. "I have shown myself to you, but you have not seen. You have no idea what adds to my happiness."

"Of course I know you Beth. We have been together since childhood."

112

"In our childhood we stood together," she said, "but somewhere along the way you grew larger than the rest of us. I cannot live and grow in your shadow. When I am with you, I only shrink a little more each day."

"But Beth, you belong with me."

"No, Buceph," she said, gently taking his hand. "I belong to myself, and I belong here. If you try to make me into someone you think I should be, it will put a wall between us. I cannot be what you try to make of me. I can only be what I am."

"Beth, you are the most important thing in the world to me," Buceph pleaded. "I will protect you. I will keep you safe from harm. I will do anything for you."

"How much more would you do than you have already done, Buceph?" Beth asked with growing impatience. "Would you destroy a rose for fear that its thorn might prick me? Would you dam a river for fear that I might get my sandals wet? Would you kill a bird for fear that its song might disturb my sleep? My dear Buceph, I fear that your cloak of protection would be so tightly wrapped that I would suffocate."

It was obvious that there was no use pleading with Beth. Her resolve was firm. "And I suppose Dunston. . . ." He turned his face away and squeezed tears from his swollen eyes.

Beth stared at the ground. "He accepts me as I am, Buceph. He has always been there for me."

Buceph clenched his fists, turned, and walked away rather than doing something foolish he would later regret.

Chapter 20

Grief and Obsession

Buceph returned to Bonaventure alone, and numbly went through the ceremony which restored him to his rightful place as monarch. He appeared humble and grateful as he tolerated the accolades which were heaped upon him, but the pain of Beth's loss clouded his victory.

The ceremonies were concluded by noon, and Buceph slipped away and headed up the trail toward the Promontory Point to be alone for a time. Beth was still very much on his mind. As he trudged the path alone, head down, eyes focused only on his next step, he took the crystal from around his neck almost without thinking. When he reached the point, he took a deep breath, closed his eyes and held it high in the air. When the Guide appeared, no words were spoken. Buceph followed, silently, obediently.

It was dark when they reached the Ascetic's cave.   The old one was sitting in his tranquil spot by the fire and Buceph dropped himself despondently into the old stump chair. "I have lost Beth," he began. "She was mine and now she no longer belongs to me. She has left me for Dunston."

"You have not lost her, for you did not possess her," replied the Ascetic. "To love something means that it does not belong to you. If it belongs to you, it means you do not love it."

"But I did love her," Buceph protested. "I have always placed her before me."

"And when you did, did she not stand in your way?"

Buceph stared blankly, then hung his head. "I only wished to protect her. I wanted to shield her from the ugliness."

"To be protected is to live with secrets and lies," the Ascetic said. "People find no comfort in dishonesty."

"Are you saying that it is wrong to try to make someone happy when they are sad, safe when they are afraid, comforted when they are in pain?"

"I am saying that you were dishonest to keep her out of your way. When you impose your solutions upon another's challenges you say to them that they are incapable of finding their own solutions. You say to them that they are unacceptable."

"But my intentions were only to make her happy," replied Buceph defensively.

"When your own happiness depends upon the happiness of another, it naturally follows that making the other happy means a great deal."

"You are saying that I wanted to please her only to ensure my own security?" Buceph said indignantly. "How could you suggest that I was so selfish?"

"Many selfish things are disguised as gifts," replied the Ascetic.

Buceph seated himself on the ground between the chair and the fire. Avoiding the Ascetic's gaze, he nervously picked up a handful of cool ashes from the edge of the fire. "She never told me. She always said that she wanted for nothing."

"How very sad," the Ascetic said. "To have nothing left to desire leaves a terrible longing for desire."

"Then I do not understand what she needed from me," Buceph said, puzzled by the Ascetic's reply.

"She needed only what everyone needs from another--the freedom to think and feel without being judged, to speak and act without being criticized, to live and be without being controlled. It is freedom that binds people together."

Buceph poured the fine ash nervously to and fro, hand to hand. A tear rolled off his cheek as the Ascetic continued. "That which one truly loves must be free to remain close. Even the ashes in your hand when held too tightly escape your grasp. It is only when something is no longer struggling to be free that it can choose to remain."

After a few moments Buceph spoke again. "I suppose it is not so hard to understand, now that I see myself as she sees me," he sobbed, his tears making small beads of mud in the fine sift. "I held her too tightly out of my own need and gave no thought to the needs she might have. I took her for granted when I was away from her. Then when I returned, I clung to her until she could no longer bear the weight of me. She must have thought I did not care."

"People often care too much about the things which mean nothing and too little about the things which mean everything."

"I must make things right with her. What must I do?"

"Sometimes the kindest thing one can do for someone we have hurt is to leave them alone."

Buceph sobbed uncontrollably. Dawn was breaking. The Guide appeared at Buceph's shoulder, signaling that another visit had come to a close.

By noon, Buceph was safely back at his home in Bonaventure. Exhausted from his encounter, he flopped into his bed and slept through the remainder of the day.

In the days that followed, Buceph did as the Ascetic suggested and left Beth alone while focusing his energies on his duties and the rebuilding of Oxymora. In time he grew skilled at the high level political and economic postures required to maintain relations with Malthus and Carpathia, and the people idolized him. The turmoil and chaos subsided and peace was being maintained painlessly. Buceph had his hand in every aspect of growth and development of Oxymoran society and prosperity was steadily on the rise.

Five years passed, and Buceph had remained faithful to his vow that he would leave Beth alone. But now, as the demands of his office eased with the increasing prosperity, his mind was frequently occupied with thoughts of Beth and Kimrey. Soon, he found himself agonizing in loneliness. His son was five years old and Buceph had not taken part in his life.

The more he indulged his emptiness for Beth, the more his obsession for her grew. A fire was being kindled in his soul which rivaled his passion for conquering Malthus. His every waking moment was spent scheming, plotting, planning ways to get Beth and Kimrey back in his life.

The Council was becoming increasingly concerned over Buceph's escalating stress. His lack of attention to pressing problems was impeding their progress, and their goading and prodding had done little to recapture his focus. When they had exhausted all other avenues, they appointed the Elder from Trada to approach Buceph with a solution. "Buceph, the Council is concerned about the overwhelming duties which have befallen you," the Elder began. "We need your talent for handling foreign affairs, and we fear that too many mundane duties are interfering with that important function."

Buceph was attentive, and far more open than the Elder expected. "And what does the Council of Elders suggest?" he asked.

"We propose the creation of a new position in our government--a Chief of the Council to be responsible for routine domestic affairs so that you will be free to concentrate your talents where they are most needed. All other governments have such an individual who handles affairs of state--why not Oxymora?"

"Perhaps you are right," Buceph quickly agreed.

"Well, then," the surprised Elder continued, "shall we proceed and select such a person?"

"I will concede to your proposition on one condition--that Dunston be appointed to the post."

The Elder paused. "I cannot see that that would pose any problems for the Council," he finally replied, after carefully considering Buceph's condition. " His sacrifices for Oxymora have not been forgotten. But why Dunston? Everyone knows that there has been a longstanding rift between the two of you."

"He is the best man for the job," was Buceph's only reply, and the Elder did not question him further.

The Council enthusiastically endorsed Dunston to fill the post, and they wasted no time in dispatching a messenger requesting Dunston's presence in Bonaventure. Dunston could hardly refuse such a high request and, true to his character, he arrived in Bonaventure at the appointed time and appeared before the Council.

"With Buceph's approval, we have created a new post in our government," the Elder from Trada began. "We are going to appoint a Chief of the Council who will assume many of Buceph's domestic duties, and you have been selected by the Council to assume those duties."

"And may I ask why I was chosen?" Dunston asked.

The Elder squirmed in his seat, shooting nervous glances toward the other Council members, hesitating before he answered. "Buceph insisted that it be you who fills the post," he finally replied.

Dunston looked about the room, trying to gauge their attitudes.

"And does the Council agree that I am the best man for the job?"

"Oh, yes!" the Elder quickly replied. "We hold you in the highest regard."

Dunston paused again. "Then I shall not refuse your requests," he said, though he suspected Buceph's motives were ignoble, that the appointment was shrouded in duty and honor to conceal some ulterior plan.

Nevertheless, Dunston was most gracious in his acceptance, and throughout the inauguration ceremony, he was guarded but cordial with Buceph. He wished to impart a clear message that it was purely out of duty to Oxymora rather than loyalty to him that he had accepted this honor.

Chapter 21

Victory Over Malthus

Dunston assumed his position and performed his duties well, proving himself equal to the demands of his new office, though he assumed an air of caution in his dealings with Buceph, ever watching, ever waiting, ever vigilant. Buceph, on the other hand, was quite pleased with himself--Beth and Kimrey had moved to Bonaventure. It was a step in the right direction, but Buceph still saw little of them, and so he settled into a life of restless discontent while Dunston and Beth raised Kimrey quietly in his shadow.

Seven years passed. Buceph and Dunston had long since learned to cooperate with one another in matters of state and to avoid one another in matters personal. It was a rare day when they spoke face to face, so it came as quite a surprise to Buceph when the chamber guard interrupted his musings one day with the announcement that Dunston wished to talk with him.

Dunston shuffled across the floor, eyes sad, head hung in shame. "What is it my old friend?" Buceph asked, placing his hand on Dunston's drooped shoulder.

"I am tired, Buceph," Dunston replied. "My hopes and dreams have died and I have lost all hope that our homeland will ever become the home for the Outlanders the Prophecy promised. I have always been willing to give my all for Oxymora, but I am not sure my investment has been a wise one."

"You are still angry with my decisions," Buceph said, "but you know that we had no choice but to compromise. Is it not clear to you that we are better off under our alliance with Malthus than we were under their rule?"

119

The Keeper of the Trees

"I see only a pit of writhing snakes, vying for top of the pile," Dunston replied. "Our politicians are using their position for personal gain. Those who have amassed much are wracking themselves day and night in search of ways to amass more while those who have amassed little strive to displace those who have amassed much."

"But look at the progress we have made, Dunston. Malthus provides us with tools, weapons, adornments; we have a ready market for our copper; we even have surplus grain, wood, produce, and pelts to trade. It seems to me that we have compromised but little. Our interdependence has proved to be mutually beneficial and a fair solution for both lands."

Dunston shook his head. "I'm not so sure that we are so much better off, and I'm not even sure that our agreement is mutually beneficial. Our people have lost their integrity. They pride themselves on taking advantage of the Malthusians. Our merchants boast of price gouging, our woodsmen boast of selling the second grade lumber and keeping the best, our farmers boast of keeping the best grain and selling that which still has chaff."

"But Dunston, there is evidence of progress everywhere. Speed and efficiency have replaced our crude ways. Our land is prosperous; the people have plenty. Oxymora sails as smoothly as a well-trimmed ship."

"That may be true," Dunston replied, "but it holds no more of life than a wooden hull. Our dependence on Malthus has made us a performance society, the worth of its members measured by gains and losses. Our people have become vengeful, greedy, dishonest. I have looked for the goodness, the kindness, the generosity which built our land, but it is no longer to be found."

"Perhaps the people are what we taught them to be," Buceph said, staring out the window.

"I'm afraid you are right, Buceph," Dunston sighed. "I suppose it is my expectations which are causing my pain. It is about my hopes and dreams for our land. They have died and I grieve their passing. I am weary of chasing my ideals and I am weary of my grief."

Buceph continued to gaze out the window. "And I of mine," he replied. "I too hold deep resentments over our dependence on Malthus. I suppose all living things resent that on which they must depend."

"But most do not find it reason enough to hurt themselves over it," Dunston said.

Just then, Oberon burst into Buceph's chambers unannounced. With a great grin, he rushed across the room, grabbed Buceph and hugged him. "Vistar is dead," he shouted. "You, my friend, are the new Monarch of Malthus."

Buceph's eyes widened; his jaw dropped. Dunston stared, eyebrows raised in expectation and confusion. Their puzzled looks prompted Oberon to explain. "Your mother was Vistar's only heir and you are her only heir. The Council of Malthus has dispatched me to inform you that Vistar's throne and all he acquired has befallen you. You must sail with me to Malthus and claim your throne."

Tears filled Buceph's eyes. "Perhaps this is the moment, Dunston," he said, turning to his old friend. "*This* is the victory that our success is destined to follow!" he said, choking back tears. "The principles the Ascetic showed me truly *do* work."

Dunston smiled skeptically, and Buceph looked back toward Oberon. "Of course I will sail with you to Malthus."

"Good!" said Oberon. "Then we shall begin our voyage when the moon is full and the tide high."

When Oberon had departed, Buceph donned his cape and set out toward the Promontory Point. Anxious to report this windfall to the Ascetic, he fairly thrust the crystal in the air. The Guide appeared as always, and they began their journey up the mountain.

When they arrived at the cave, Buceph seated himself and confidently began his account. "For years, I have devoted all my waking hours and many of my dreams to achieve victory over Malthus and now, through ironic fate, I am its Monarch. We have our victory."

"And now it is time for you to learn to endure that victory," the Ascetic said. "The true test of your character shall lie in the way you live with that victory. It is a far greater challenge than embracing loss."

Buceph wrinkled his brow. "I find it hard to imagine that our victory shall be more to bear than our defeat," he said. "Perhaps we will not find our freedom so burdensome."

"It will only become burdensome if it carries with it the exercise of power."

"But is it not the exercise of power that will keep us free?"

"You cannot force people to be free," the Ascetic replied.

Buceph's face grew taut with frustration. "I have valued freedom above all things. I have risked all, worked tirelessly, sacrificed much to achieve that freedom and if it takes power to sustain it then I shall exercise power."

"Freedom enforced by power is not freedom," the Ascetic said. "People become slaves to that kind of freedom the moment they are required to protect it."

"But there is no man, no group, no country posing any challenge to our success," Buceph said.

"The threat is not from without, but from within," the Ascetic replied. "The threat is complacency, for it lurks in success and failure lies in complacency."

"I shall no longer accept failure," Buceph said. "If our freedom does not lie in power, our success surely does."

"Power is not success," the Ascetic said, "nor does success have anything to do with power. That is something you should understand better than anyone, Buceph. You once acquired power by simply putting anger to work, but it did not bring you success."

"You are right, Ascetic, but now we will possess great riches as well as power."

"It is more common that riches possess men, than men riches," the Ascetic said. "It is what one becomes that counts, Buceph, not what one acquires. There is weariness in abundance."

"It was you who taught me that I must surrender to win," Buceph snapped. "I did and I won, and now I intend to see that Oxymora profits from that victory just as Malthus profitted from their victory over Oxymora."

"You will do unto them as they have done unto you?" asked the Ascetic.

"Is that not The Way of victory?" Buceph replied. "Is it not right to take from others as they have taken from us?"

"That which you take from others is not of you, from you, or for you," the Ascetic replied. "Only as you give back what you have taken, do you make room for things of our own. *That* is The Way of victory."

Buceph squirmed in his seat. "Did you not tell my father that success can only follow victory?"

"It is true that success follows victory, but I think you have missed the point. There is no greater defeat than being powerful and in control, for people are always mastered by that which they try to control."

Buceph's lips grew thin over gritted teeth. His eyes narrowed. "We deserve all that we shall gain. We have earned our right to these privileges and I intend to see that Oxymora enjoys them."

"It is a privilege to have rights," the Ascetic replied, "but to gain what others have lost is not a right. Rights do not come from being in power. Rights are only rights when they apply to all."

"And just what rights should I accord the Malthusians?"

"It is not yours to accord them anything, for the Malthusian's rule you still," the Ascetic answered. Buceph's eyes widened, his eyebrows lifted, his chin dropped. "How can you say that the land I now rule, rules me?"

"Are they not even now controlling your feelings and actions?"

Buceph was confounded, and then it struck him. "It is my anger that I have not conquered, isn't it? I shall not have succeeded until I have won that victory."

"I am happy that you finally see," the Ascetic said. "Victory over self is the most difficult to achieve."

"But if I lose my anger, the Malthusians will not fear me. I might lose the respect I now command."

"Fear is not respect nor respect fear, and respect cannot be commanded, it must be earned," replied the Ascetic.

"Then just how do you propose I rid myself of my anger toward them?"

"Look into their hearts," the Ascetic replied. "Perhaps you will find enough pain and sorrow and suffering there to dissolve it."

Chapter 22

A Look at the Enemy

By the time the moon had reached its fullness, Buceph had set his affairs in order and delegated his duties to Dunston. He was ready to face Malthus.

For two weeks at sea, little was spoken between Oberon and Buceph. Oberon went about the business of tending the ship while Buceph spent most of his time alone in his cabin. Day and night he pondered the Ascetic's words, and he wondered what sort of reception he might receive in Malthus, though he was fairly certain it would not be a warm one.

It was noon on the fifteenth day when Oberon docked *The Adventurer* at the eastern port of Malthus. Judging by the size of the crowd which gathered, Buceph was not sure whether he was facing a welcoming party or a lynch mob, but it soon became apparent that the crowd considered Oberon a familiar and welcome sight. "Oberon, you never cease to amaze me," he said. "You make no bones about your self-serving ways, and yet you have never made an enemy of any man."

"Your father never understood me either," Oberon chuckled. "To me it is quite simple. Rivalry requires two parties with differing views. I hold no particular views, therefore I cannot participate."

Buceph laughed aloud, shaking his head. Oberon moved to the starboard deck and whistled for the attention of the crowd. They fell silent. "This is your new Monarch," he announced. "This is Buceph of Oxymora, son of Anna and rightful heir to Vistar's legacy."

Buceph's surprise was not easily contained when a rousing cheer rose from the crowd. Nonetheless, he was most gracious in accepting his leadership.

Dusk was approaching as they arrived at Vistar's estate, and the twilight lent an ominous appearance to the massive compound. They entered the gate, strolled up the crooked path to the main house, opened the massive wooden door, and stepped inside. Buceph stood in the atrium and looked down the hollow hallway. Finally, Oberon broke the silence. "What is it, Buceph? What's troubling you?"

"I must admit, Oberon, I did not expect so warm a welcome from so recent an enemy. Can it be that they hold no anger, no resentment, no blame?"

"You are the only one who finds those things of any value, Buceph," Oberon said bluntly. "They wish only to live their lives in peace and let the rest of the world do the same. They have been dealt more than their share of pain."

"I fear that I have not much sympathy for their pain, Oberon."

"Just what do you really know of the Malthusians, Buceph?" Oberon asked. "Your hatred of them had been powerful and enduring, but do you know what it is you hate?"

"I know that they raped and slaughtered our people and burned our villages!" Buceph snapped. "I know that they are pompous, aggressive, greedy. . . ."

Oberon shook his head. "Why is it that the good is never remembered and the bad never forgotten. It is true there was a time when the Malthusians placed their faith in wealth and power, but those things failed them. The people of Malthus turned to higher things long ago. It is Oxymora that has become pompous, aggressive, and greedy."

"Do you mean to say that these people do not lust and clamor for our copper?"

"They never did, Buceph. What happened between Malthus and Oxymora was never the wish of the Malthusian people. For the most part, they could care less about Oxymoran copper, for it has done little to improve their lives. The wealth produced by your copper fell into the hands of the few who governed. The Malthusian people place more value on people and relationships than on power and wealth."

"It is The Way!" Buceph said in astonishment. "They follow The Way! My mother was banished from here for following The Way!"

"Actually, it was your mother's banishment that triggered a quiet rebellion. Anna was much beloved, and these gentle people could not abide

125

The Keeper of the Trees

Vistar's decision to banish his own daughter for the sake of power and wealth. They were wise enough to see that any system which separates its followers cannot long endure."

"And are they not banished for such practices just as my mother was banished?"

Oberon chuckled. "Malthus abandoned that age-old practice years ago."

"But what about Vistar?" Buceph asked. "I can hardly imagine that he would sanction such practices."

"To understand that, you have to understand Vistar. He always valued wealth and power and he was exceedingly shrewd. He knew that those who follow The Way did not value wealth and power and posed no threat to the accumulation of his riches."

"And so he allowed them to follow The Way?"

"He not only allowed it, he encouraged it," Oberon said. "He logically and rightly concluded that if everyone followed The Way, he would be free to hoard all he desired. People who followed The Way did not compete with him for power and wealth. It was only the greed of the Oxymoran people that matched his underhanded tactics lie for lie."

Buceph hung his head and reflected for a moment. "If what you say is true, then many Malthusians were following The Way when they attacked our land. It makes no sense."

"There will always be those few who hold to their faith in power and wealth regardless of what the many believe. It is true that when Vistar ordered the attacks on Oxymora, most Malthusians were following The Way, but in all lands there will always be the Hedons. You know that, Buceph. Did you not build your rebel band with Hedons when you attacked the Malthusians? That was a battle between Hedons, not a conflict between Oxymora and Malthus."

Buceph nodded his head. "And I have no doubt that Vistar rewarded his Elite Guard generously, just as we did our rebel band," he replied, "but we also had the support of the people."

"And that is where you differ from Vistar. The people of Malthus had no such power. They were in no position to sanction or negate the decisions of their leaders. They had grown so weary of squabbles that they grew indifferent to their government. Few even knew of Vistar's actions."

Buceph looked pensively out over the city. "They live in near-poverty. They have such meager possessions."

"It is true that they have little, but they find it enough."

"It seems that our greed and corruption have hurt them far worse than they have hurt us. Just what do they expect from me, Oberon?"

"You are still suspicious, my friend. They want nothing from you, for they believe that you have nothing of real value to offer them. From what they know of you, they see you as being no different from Vistar, and they have learned how to live comfortably under his kind of rule."

For Buceph, being compared so blithely to Vistar was like being kicked in the stomach. He wanted to throw up, but swallowed hard and continued. "Do they know of the Prophecy?"

"They know," replied Oberon. "And in spite of everything that has happened between Oxymora and Malthus, you are their hope, not because of your rule, but because of your link to the Prophecy. They are willing to endure any pain you may inflict upon them in order to realize its promise."

"Has my wrath done them no harm at all?"

"Your anger, my friend, belongs only to you," Oberon replied. "They do not allow themselves the indignity of yielding to such petty annoyances. They only pity you, Buceph. They include you in their prayers."

"How dare they think me pitiful!" Buceph snapped. "I have been their staunch adversary. I am to be feared and respected, not pitied."

"You are angry because you do not control their feelings, but you have no control over them. The object of your anger refuses to permit your anger to harm them."

"But do they not resent their lack?"

"Is it not obvious to you that they do not experience lack?" Oberon asked.

Buceph's face reddened, his lips pursed. "Then if they are so content with their meager existence, I will let them have their due."

Oberon hung his head in despair. "I was afraid that would be your attitude. You have not yet put your resentments behind you, have you Buceph?"

"They have too long been the enemy of all that Oxymora was intended to be."

"And just what was Oxymora intended to be, Buceph?"

"What do you mean, Oberon? You know that it was intended to be the home for the Outlanders, the haven for the lost."

"I know only what I have seen," replied Oberon.

"And what have you seen?" Buceph asked.

"I have seen Oxymora, once welcoming of all, close its shores to outcasts from Malthus while Malthus welcomed outcasts from Oxymora. I have seen Oxymora scorn The Way in favor of wealth and power while Malthus shunned wealth and power in favor of The Way. One might even wonder if it is not Malthus that is more of a home for the Outlanders than Oxymora."

Buceph clinched his fists and shook with rage. Truth had penetrated his wall of denial. Then, suddenly, he softened, and was quiet for a time. "It is ironic, Oberon," he lamented. "The Ascetic says that we must all become what we despise before we can understand it."

Neither of them spoke for a time, then Oberon continued. "What will you do, Buceph, now that you are their ruler?"

Buceph did not reply.

In the days that followed, Buceph toured the marketplace, visited the copper foundry, met with the Advisory Council, and everywhere he went he was received with honor and respect. Contrary to his belief, he found the Malthusians to be a kind and gentle people. He sensed not a hint of animosity, and soon he moved freely among them without fear. He spent his days learning their laws, observing their customs, assessing their economy and his nights behind closed doors in conference with Oberon.

Oberon watched and waited, hoping for any sign that the warmth of the Malthusian people would melt Buceph's icy shell, but Buceph remained coolly unemotional, studying, analyzing, evaluating.

When the time to return to Oxymora drew near, Buceph announced that there would be a proclamation on the day of their departure. When the day came, a great crowd gathered about *The Adventurer* and awaited Buceph's appearance.

With the sun directly overhead, Buceph stepped to the bow with Oberon by his side. "People of Malthus," he began. "Your hospitality has charmed me and I intend to see to it that Malthus and Oxymora shall henceforth live in peace, one with the other."

The crowd listened intently, but with smiling faces as Buceph continued. "As you know, my interests lie in Oxymora. Since my duties require my presence there, I shall not be governing you directly. Instead, I shall appoint a Governor. Eventually you shall be ruled by my son, Kimrey, but he has not yet reached his Time of Wisdom, and that shall not occur until the next coming of the Star. Until then, I thought it important to select someone you know and love. Until then you shall be governed by Oberon."

Chatter rustled through the crowd. When the hum died down, Buceph continued. "For now I must bid you goodbye. Oberon shall deliver me back to Oxymora and when he returns to you, give to him your support and acceptance. If you can give these things to me, it should be an easy matter to give them to Oberon, for he needs not nearly so much tolerance as I."

The crowd cheered and waved. Buceph had won their hearts, if not they, his. They continued cheering and waving until *The Adventurer* set sail, and Buceph gazed longingly at the horizon from the ship's stern long after Malthus had disappeared.

Oberon smiled to himself when he saw Buceph, bent over, head in hands, sobbing deeply, but he said nothing. He would give Buceph the dignity of his pain and the time and space to feel his longing for a deeper peace.

Chapter 23

A Search for Forgiveness

Two weeks later *The Adventurer* sailed around the southern tip of Oxymora and moored in Aleph's Cove. Buceph disembarked and, trying to get his legs accustomed to land once more, staggered toward the Promontory Point, crystal in hand. He was eager to report his findings to the Ascetic.

The trip up Mount Erudite with the Guide was silent as usual, and quite tiring after two weeks at sea, but Buceph felt a deep comfort about the decisions he had made. There were no looming crises, no great problems to be solved, and there was no pain. As they ascended the mountain, Buceph was unusually aware of the rocks, the streams, the ground beneath his feet, the sheer beauty of his surroundings. These things never seemed to change, and neither did the Guide nor the Ascetic. They, too, were ageless. He wondered if they had been the same when his father first met them.

When they reached the Ascetic's cave, Buceph looked at the old man through new eyes. He was more curious, more respectful, more in awe. He sat in the old stump chair, leaned back with a sigh and began. "I have been to Malthus, and there I was given the eyes to see what you have been trying to show me."

"And what is it you have seen, Buceph?" asked the Ascetic.

"I have seen that I lent great weight to the things we bore from the Malthusians, but failed to recognize what they have born from us. Perhaps we have exceeded the exacting of our due. They have been living in near poverty since our agreement with Vistar was sealed. I only knew of the injustices we suffered from that agreement. I knew nothing of those the agreement afflicted."

130

"And do you now believe that their debt is paid?"

"I do not believe that I shall ever again feel self-righteous anger without looking well to what is truly deserved."

"Is this the first time you have ever felt empathy?"

Buceph cocked his head and looked into the Ascetic's questioning eyes. "I suppose I do not know the meaning of empathy," he said.

"Empathy is nothing more than the vision that enables you to see things from another's viewpoint. It is conceding to others the right to do things in their own way. It is giving others the same right to make mistakes that you have been given. It is respecting differences. Of all character traits you may possess, empathy is the greatest."

Buceph nervously chewed his lip. "Then I suppose I have never had any empathy until now," he said. "I have known only anger and it has driven me to seek only victory and revenge."

"And now that you have your victory and can inflict your revenge, what have you won and how shall you choose to hurt them?"

"I thought my anger had already hurt them, but it has done them no harm at all," Buceph replied. "I have won nothing."

"It must have been terrible to learn that you had spent all that energy for no purpose. Is there any part of your life that you did not give them? Did you keep any part of it for yourself?"

Buceph hung his head. "I fear not," he said. "I have allowed them to claim my life. I gave them my thoughts, I let them control my feelings, my actions were directed by theirs. I gave my youth to defeating them and my adulthood to outwitting them."

"Then your anger has caused you to become their victim."

Buceph thought for a long while on the Ascetic's comment. "Perhaps victor and victim are one and the same. It was an easy matter to absolve myself and blame my adversary."

"Perhaps you absolved your adversary and blamed yourself," replied the Ascetic, "else you would not have punished yourself so."

"Punished myself?"

"Is that not what you have been doing, Buceph?" the Ascetic asked. "Has not your anger at their past deeds been the source of your pain?"

"Why, yes, it has," Buceph admitted. "In nourishing my anger I gave up my contentment."

The Keeper of the Trees

"When you begin to nourish your contentment, you will begin to give up your anger," replied the Ascetic.

"And just how is it that I am to do that?"

"Contentment is gained in direct proportion to the rights you give others to be your equal in foolishness," the Ascetic replied. "There is no honor in victory if it only makes you a superior fool."

"It is only now that I am beginning to see my foolishness," Buceph said. "I only wanted to do what was right."

"The only reason to label things *right* or *wrong* is to justify harming others," replied the Ascetic. "The Way does not speak of right or wrong. It speaks only of consequences."

"And the consequences that both Malthus and Oxymora have had to pay have been largely the result of my own actions," Buceph admitted. "The things that I blamed the Malthusians for doing, I did; the things I blamed them for being, I was." He sat quietly for a time staring far out to sea.

"When we impose our way on others, believing we know what they need, we most often harm those we intend to help," replied the Ascetic.

"Dunston spoke to me of his concerns about our homeland before I left for Malthus, but I tried to deny that anything was wrong." Buceph hung his head. "To do so would be to admit that I had failed." He turned and looked up into the Ascetic's kind eyes. "But after visiting Malthus I could no longer be convinced by my own lies."

"One cannot see what is obvious when standing too close," the Ascetic said, "for we get caught up in, and become part of, the thing we are looking upon. When there is distance, one can appreciate the whole. Just what is it you see now, Buceph?"

"I see that Oxymora is filled with greed and lusts and struggles for power," Buceph replied. "I would wager that even as we speak, many are plotting new ways to exploit the new relationship with Malthus. The things they once valued have been supplanted by intolerance, prejudice, impatience, and judgmental attitudes."

"You have built this house with your own hands," replied the Ascetic. "Do not blame it for not being a home. You speak of the people as if they are different from you. In so doing, are you not even now, showing your intolerance of those who are intolerant, showing your prejudice against those who are prejudiced, being impatient with those who lack patience, being judgmental of those who are judgmental?"

132

Buceph hung his head once more. "Perhaps there shall never be victory for me," he lamented. "Perhaps I am searching for a destination on a circle which has no beginning and no end."

"It is a true dilemma when failure causes you to try harder and trying harder causes you to fail."

"All the more reason I should understand my purpose," Buceph said, "for then I will know just what direction to take."

"Very well," the Ascetic said. "Then you shall know your purpose. Your purpose is to experience the defeat of victory so the Enlightened One will know not to seek your kind of victory, and you are fulfilling that purpose very well. You do not know it, but you have already laid most of the groundwork. Perhaps someday, with distance, you will be able to see the larger plan and the gift you are giving."

"And just what gift is that?" Buceph asked skeptically.

"The purpose for you and for Aleph has been to map paths for the Keeper of the Trees to avoid," the Ascetic said.

"That is hardly a purpose I would have chosen for myself," Buceph said indignantly.

"That is why it was not up to you to choose it," the Ascetic replied, "nor was it up to Aleph to choose his purpose. Aleph mapped out the failure that lies in success and you are mapping out the defeat that lies victory."

"I have spent my life fighting to build and preserve a home for the Outlanders of the world. I gave up wondering long ago about the Trees, for my father told me that they were unfathomable. Just what am I supposed to do now? Just where will my victory lie?"

"The only way to gain your victory is to let go of all things which keep you in a position of control," replied the Ascetic. "You can give up your fight anytime you choose, for you have won your defeat."

Buceph's eyebrows lifted in confusion. "You are talking about relinquishing all the things I have spent my life achieving!"

"To stay in control means that you believe that it is your place to be protective of others, to control their thoughts, affect their feelings and direct their actions," the Ascetic said. "What if they do follow your leading, Buceph? Do you suppose that they will become as happy as you? Do you suppose they will become as humble as you? Do you suppose they will become as flawless as you? Do you suppose they will manage the new world as well as you have managed the old one?"

"Trying to stay in control of Beth is what destroyed our relationship."

"When you try to adjust people to your direction by doing things for them on their behalf, you may ease *your* discomfort, but it is usually at their expense. When you stop arranging outcomes, you permit people to learn from their consequences and thus affect their own destiny."

"And if I do, what would become of my dream for the home for the Outlanders?" Buceph protested. "What would become of Oxymora?"

"To free yourself of Oxymora would be to free Oxymora," the Ascetic replied. "but that can only happen when you realize that it is not your place to direct or criticize or regulate anyone or anything."

"But that would mean that I no longer care."

"To let go does not mean you stop caring," the Ascetic said. "It means that you learn to *care about* rather than to *care for*. It means that you learn to treat Oxymora as you have treated your son. Because you care about Kimrey, you have let someone else care for him."

Buceph frowned and looked toward the ground. "Kimrey will soon be coming to spend his Time of Reason with me and I fear that I have nothing to offer him."

"You can still shape your gift to your son," the Ascetic said. "The choice is up to you. It has always been up to you. Go into the Dark Forest alone and make your choice. You can wallow in self-pity or you can stop blaming others and begin making the most of yourself. You can live with your anger, or you can learn to forgive the past and live and grow for the future. You can live with worry and frustration or you can take each day as it comes and cherish it."

Chapter 24

The Lion

Buceph did go into the Dark Forest, but soon his courage waned. He had been here before, but never alone, and now he understood why. The mist which hung among the trees cast a gray, heavy atmosphere over the moss-covered branches. The few beams of light which penetrated the higher branches tried to pierce the fog, but were absorbed into it before they touched the ground. And the silence! Where were all the animals, the birds, the insects? He had never faced anything so completely alone, and there was something very unreal about the forest.

All day, he wandered aimlessly, sometimes running, sometimes falling to rest for a few moments before carrying on. He desperately wanted out, but no border could he find. By evening, his frantic attempt to flee had left him too exhausted to fight sleep. He gathered himself a pile of leaves for a bed and snuggled down among them, and soon he was fast asleep. And as he slept a cloud appeared, and from the cloud emerged a lion.

Buceph sat bolt upright, startled by the apparition. He rubbed his eyes but it did not go away. "You frighten me," Buceph said, shrinking from the powerful beast. "Who are you?"

"I am The Life That Is come to you as your Spirit of Experience," said the lion. "Experience is always frightening because it is so powerful."

"Experience has done little but illuminate my weaknesses," Buceph said.

"People find me in their weakness, not in their strength," said the lion.

"Then I should know you well, for my life has certainly been one of weakness," Buceph said.

"Then why do you not know me well?" asked the lion.

"Perhaps I have not sought you because I fear your power and your wrath."

"But I have no anger to be appeased," said the lion. "I am not after you, Buceph. I am for you."

"Very well, if you are powerful like a lion, then why do you let bad things happen to good people? Why do you condemn little children go hungry while greedy old men grow fat? Why do you allow innocents to die while rascals live in revelry? How can you be trusted?"

"If I were what you think me, I would not trust me either," said the lion. "People cannot trust what they fear, nor can they fear what they trust. What do you trust, Buceph?"

"I trust my knowledge and my reason," Buceph replied. "I tried praying to you, but I never got the answers I needed. I suppose my petitions were not the right kind."

"I do not wait for the right kind of prayer," said the lion. "You do not control my actions or conjure my presence or invoke my power by praying rightly."

"Then what is the purpose of prayer?"

"It is not to change me, but to change you," replied the lion, "for I am not the problem."

"Then your purpose is only to make changes inside us?" asked Buceph.

"That is the only miracle I perform," replied the lion. "I offer inside solutions to outside problems."

"Then do you never intervene in man's affairs?" Buceph asked. "Do you make no changes in the world at all?"

"It is my job to make changes in you. It is your job to make changes in the world. What I offer is inspiration. It is up to you to create what you will."

"Then I must start by living a life of goodness and doing what is right."

"To be always right is to be doing something wrong and there is much bad which comes from always being good," said the lion. "Had you lived a life of right and good, you would have missed the adventures necessary to the awakening of your spirit. Instead, you have gained the humility and the wisdom which doing right and being good could never have brought you."

"I though you were always on the side of right and good," Buceph said.

"Right and good exist on all sides. I never choose one group over another, nor do I favor one person over another. I do not dispense mercy to some at the expense of justice for others. I do not help some and hurt others."

"Then doing right and being good must be about entering the Place of Eternal Comfort."

"There are many who believe that their purity will earn them a high station, but where will they be if entering the Place of Eternal Comfort is about overcoming selfishness? What if it is about the kindness that carries with it no thought of reward?"

Buceph chuckled. "They will be left outside, standing in their goodness."

"Eternal comfort is not for sale or for trade," the lion continued, "and if you spend your time here concerning yourself with how to get to there, you have missed the point. Your purpose here is to be concerned about the place on earth others should have."

Buceph stared pensively out to sea. "Those who follow The Way speak of a spiritual experience. I have longed to know just what is it they have found?"

"Spiritual experience is most often gained through worldly experience, for people are but spiritual beings exploring worldly experiences. But it is not necessarily a magical time or a memorable event. Spiritual experience comes in much the same way that job experience comes--with repetitive practice. It is about taking a little, then adding a little to it. When you do that with regularity, the *little* soon becomes something grand."

Buceph was quiet for a long while. "If only I had your wisdom with me," he finally said. "Will I see you again?"

"You will glimpse me in moments when everything you are is the same as everything you think you are. You will feel me stirring within you in moments when everything you do is the same as everything you say you do."

"Then how am I to serve you now?"

"There is no higher service than doing for others solely for the love of doing it," replied the lion. "Help others see how to live together and you will be letting The Life That Is smile through."

"Then it is about living together in peace?"

"Yes, it is about living together in peace," replied the lion.

Buceph was quiet for a time. "There are those who say they know you. Might I come to know you as well?"

"Each time you reveal what you know of yourself to what you know of The Life That Is, more of both shall be revealed to you. It is honesty with self and others that reveals the reality of The Life That Is within you." With that, the lion disappeared back into the cloud.

The vision stayed with Buceph throughout the following day. It would not leave him. It played over and over in his mind as he wandered aimlessly through an endless sea of trees.

By nightfall he stumbled onto the path which led him from the forest. He dropped to his knees and kissed the ground, then jumped to his feet and set out toward Bonaventure.

Chapter 25

My Son, My Shame

Buceph returned to his duties a changed man. His face was relaxed, his demeanor calm, his disposition mellow. He was quiet, reflective, at peace. And, with Malthus under Oberon's able leadership, and most of Oxymora's affairs being handled by Dunston, he began to take a less prominent role in government affairs.

Dunston was more than grateful for Buceph's seemingly remarkable transformation, though he remained guarded and distant. But Kimrey's Time of Reason was at hand and according to tradition, Buceph would take an active role in his son's life during this time. Dunston knew that he and Buceph would have to face this issue sooner or later, and so he watched, waited, looking for the most advantageous time to approach him.

One beautiful spring morning Dunston followed Buceph to the Promontory Point. As Buceph settled into his solitude, Dunston approached quietly. "Buceph," he called softly. "I do not wish to invade your aloneness, but I wish to speak with you privately."

"Of course, Dunston, come, join me," Buceph said, holding out his hand to help Dunston up onto the rock where he sat. "The seas are calm today," Buceph said as he looked back to the open sea. "It is so very peaceful."

They sat for a moment looking out to the horizon and then Dunston broke the silence. "Buceph," he began, "it frightens me when I do not know what you are thinking and feeling. What happened to you in Malthus?"

Buceph paused briefly, smiling. "I saw that Malthus, our long-hated adversary, has become the beacon to the lost that Oxymora was intended to be and I realized that something was very wrong with my dream. The only thing I know at this moment is that I must stop doing what I have been doing."

"There is an urgent issue at hand," Dunston continued. "Kimrey will soon be twelve. His Time of Reason will soon be entrusted to you and will be spent under your direction. Have you given thought to the gravity of that responsibility?"

"I have given thought to little else, Dunston," Buceph replied. "I spend my days here pondering that responsibility, for I have listened in earnest to Beth's intuitions."

"He *is* the Chosen One, Buceph," Dunston insisted. "He is the reason we have endured these ordeals. He is the reason we have met these challenges."

"But if he is to be the Keeper of the Trees, a follower of The Way, what have I to offer? My whole life has been devoted to fighting and anger and control. I believed that my purpose was to preserve this haven for Outlanders. I thought I had, but even that failed. If I possessed the spiritual wisdom Kimrey will need to lift the world up and out of its ignorance and into the light, I would have used it long ago."

"You can show him The Way," Dunston suggested.

"Look, Dunston, it is obvious to me that the Keeper of the Trees will follow The Way, but I have not the wisdom of it to share. My father tried to show me The Way during my own Time of Reason, but I loathed him and refused to look at it. The Ascetic speaks of nothing else, but I often misunderstand what he tells me. I know so very little of spiritual matters."

Dunston chuckled. "Spirituality is nothing more than what you believe in. What do you believe in, Buceph?"

"That is precisely the question, Dunston," Buceph replied as he stared toward the horizon, quiet, reflective. "I know that I believe in freedom and justice and honesty and charity and. . . ."

Dunston interrupted. "All of these things are of The Way, Buceph. It's just that the means by which you tried to realize them often were not."

"I spurned The Way in favor of resentment, power, and revenge, and one can only teach what one knows. I can only give to Kimrey what I have, and I fear that my legacy shall be one of shame rather than reason."

Dunston chuckled at Buceph's self-pity. "You know that he can only learn to reason from his own failures; that his unique reason will spring from his unique experiences."

"What must I do, Dunston?"

"Speak to him, Buceph," Dunston replied. "Your aloof contemplation is giving him nothing, and better that he have unworthy gifts than no gifts at all."

"I suppose that is true," admitted Buceph. "If Kimrey is to become a reasonable man, he must suffer the joy and revel in the pain, for that is when reason is honed to its sharpest."

"The Way says that the spirit grows strong only when fully alive," Dunston said. "Beth has admonished me repeatedly for trying to change Kimrey's direction. She says that if we interfere with his mistakes, he will learn nothing. She says that his mistakes will be wisely chosen."

Buceph was quiet for a time. "Then I shall go to him and offer what I have," he said with resolve. "It is my duty, and I must trust that he will find his own way."

And so it was that when Kimrey turned twelve, Buceph took him into his home in Bonaventure. As they sat there over dinner the first evening, Buceph could not help noticing how lost, how sad, how helpless Kimrey appeared. Buceph's thoughts suddenly flashed to his own Time of Reason, and he suddenly understood all the insecurity, inadequacy, and fear his father must have felt. He could not help but pity this small, wiry, almost fragile lad.

Kimrey picked at his plate throughout dinner, eating less than half of what had been put before him. "You're eating like a bird," Buceph chuckled, trying to ease the tension a bit, but Kimrey only stared, wide-eyed and a little afraid.

"Eat your dinner and we will go to the Promontory Point," Buceph continued. "There are a few things I must discuss with you."

Kimrey's stomach went queasy. He felt as though he were in trouble for something. "I am finished, Father," he said.

They arose from the table together. Buceph placed his hand on his son's frail shoulder and guided him toward the door. They walked silently, side by side in the moonlight, and Kimrey's tension eased a bit. When they reached the point, Buceph set himself down, facing the shimmering sea, and Kimrey did likewise, sitting obediently at his father's side.

"The time has come for me to tell you of your legacy," Buceph began. "Many years ago the Ascetic foretold of a chosen one who would descend from the House of Aleph. He called this chosen one the Keeper of the Trees. He is to be our hope for the new world after the Star destroys this one."

Buceph paused and smiled down into Kimrey's somber face. "Your mother believes that it will be you."

Kimrey stared solemnly out to sea, at ease now with his father. "Perhaps I do belong in the new world," he said. "I never have felt quite at home in this one."

Buceph brushed Kimrey's comment aside. "If it is to be you, then your Time of Reason must be well spent."

"If I am the one, and the Star is to end it all soon, then why must I be groomed in government affairs at all?" Kimrey asked.

"It is a duty which befell me and it shall befall you," Buceph replied. "The Prophecy says that a haven for the lost shall herald the coming of the chosen one. That is why your grandfather established this land as a home for the Outlanders of the world."

"But hardly anyone seeks haven here anymore, Father."

Buceph smiled to himself. "I suppose that no one wishes to be saved from drowning by those who cannot swim," he said.

Kimrey chuckled for the first time since leaving his mother's house. Both were quiet for a time, then Kimrey cocked his head and spoke again. "What does the Keeper of the Trees do, Father?"

"I have no answer for that, my son," Buceph replied.

"Then what are the Trees?"

"No one knows that, either," Buceph replied. "I fear that I have little to offer you save your birthright."

"And just what right is that, Father?"

"Your birthright decrees that you shall become Monarch of our homeland, and you shall even sooner govern Malthus. Such positions carry with them both great power and grave responsibility." Buceph looked down kindly into his son's innocent face, wishing he could capture this moment and hold it in time; wishing that his son did not have to become a responsible adult.

"When I am Monarch I shall make all things fair and equal," Kimrey said. "I shall use my power unselfishly and not restrict it from anyone. It is the right thing to do."

"That is very noble, my son, but in the exercise of power, success does not always follow well-intentioned efforts. I fear that no matter what you do, your motives will be misjudged, your methods will be questioned. Lack of appreciation, personal criticism, even ridicule will be cast your way."

"What do you mean, Father?"

"No matter what your decisions, there will be those who see them favorably and those who see them unfavorably. To those who favor you, you will be a hero. To those who find disfavor with you, you will be a traitor. There will always be those who understand you and those who find you foolish."

"I already know of being misunderstood," Kimrey said.

Buceph smiled. "What could you possibly know about being misunderstood?" he asked, patting Kimrey on the head.

"I know that the other children treat me badly because I am your son. That is why I spend so much time alone."

Buceph cocked his head, eyes wide, brow raised in surprise and disbelief. "Have you no friends?" he asked.

"A few," Kimrey replied. "There's Hamer the crippled boy, and Jodie the little blind girl. They know what it is like to be different."

Buceph choked back tears. Straightening himself a bit, he struggled for something to say. "Perhaps we are meant to have adversities and should welcome them. Perhaps it is The Way to greatness."

Kimrey looked his father in the eye. "You know nothing of me, do you, Father?" he asked. "If you did, you would know that I do not seek greatness. I am ashamed of my heritage. I am ashamed of the way we have hurt people."

"Those are great concerns for such a small lad," said Buceph, a tear trickling down his cheek. "I sometimes watch you as you walk the hills alone, and I often wonder what you are thinking and feeling. Then I remember what your mother once said, that you are most at home in high places, and I believe it is true."

Buceph took the crystal from around his neck and held it out by the leather lace from which it hung. As it spun there in the sunlight, its prism-effect flashed rainbow colors across Kimrey's face and chest. "I think it is time for you to have this," Buceph said. "It is your connection to the Ascetic. When your time is right, and only you will know, grasp the crystal with both hands and hold it high above your head. The Guide will come and he will lead you to the Wise One. Better that you seek guidance from one who has something to offer you."

143

Chapter 26

From Father to Mentor

During the next four years, Kimrey remained the focus of Buceph's attention. Buceph saw to it that he was tutored in the arts to explore his creativity, trained in the military skills to build his body and enhance his alertness, groomed in the protocols of the court that he might develop a sense of justice, and provided spiritual teachings from the High Priest that he might find The Way to use what he had been given.

Under his father's tutelage, Kimrey grew into a robust youth, tall and stout, though still a bit gangly and not terribly adept at physical skills. Nonetheless, he became appropriately involved in all the activities his busy young life demanded, though Buceph sensed that much of it was an act. Kimrey wore his cloak of interest well and excelled in academics, but whenever the opportunity arose, he returned to the high country where he could be alone, contented, free.

Kimrey's sixteenth birthday was ushered in by his appointment to the Gallery of Advisors, an audience selected by the Council of Elders to represent the people. This is the way all statesmen began their careers, and Kimrey's birthright demanded that he participate.

The ceremony was stiff and formal as each new charge was paired with a mentor. Kimrey took little interest in the activities until his turn came and the Council announced that Dunston had been chosen as his mentor. Kimrey was shocked by the Council's choice, and curiosity buzzed in his head as to why they had paired him with Dunston.

When the ceremony ended, Dunston took Kimrey aside, but it was Kimrey who eagerly started the conversation. "I am delighted that you have been chosen as my mentor, but why did they choose you? They know that you guided my Time of Knowledge. They know of the rift between you and my father. Are they trying to make things worse for me?"

"Believe me, Kimrey," Dunston said, "it is not a duty I relish. I was appointed as your mentor because I am the Chief of the Council. It is the duty of my office to be mentor to the next Monarch."

"But what will this do to your relationship with my father?" Kimrey asked. "What will it do to mine?"

"Your father and I have our differences, but we have always had two things in common--we are both concerned about your future and we both have done what we believed best for you. Doing what we think is best for you now will neither heal nor deepen our wounds, nor will it tear you asunder."

Kimrey was quiet for a time. "Your differences are over my mother, aren't they Dunston?" he asked. "She says that you and my father were once as brothers, and I have seen her cry when she speaks of the three of you as children."

A tear welled in Dunston's eye. "That is your father's wound. My wound came when your father wedged his power and position between our friendship."

They were both silent for a while, then Kimrey continued. "There is something I may as well admit to you, for you will find it out soon enough anyway. The truth is that I have very little interest in matters of state."

"Your duty has nothing to do with your interests," replied Dunston. "It is just your duty."

"But why must this duty be mine?" Kimrey asked. "I do not want it."

"It is your birthright."

"My birthright is taking more of my personal rights," Kimrey complained. "My birthright has caused me nothing but difficulties and shame."

"When you have grown in reason, you will see that your birthright does not make you who you are, nor does it take anything from you," Dunston said. "The only things of real value will be the things you create on your own merit."

"Then you agree that my birthright is of no value to me?"

"Clever, Kimrey, but that is not what I said," Dunston replied. "Hopefully you will see it's value someday, when you have gained the wisdom to see it. For now, our objective is to help you connect reason to the things you know. Wisdom will come later."

"You give me but little credit," Kimrey said. "I have already endured my Time of Reason for four years now. I already know many of the things which should be done to eliminate the greed among our politicians and improve conditions for our workers."

"Yes, yes; I'm sure you do," replied Dunston, brushing Kimrey's comment aside, "Everyone has answers, but questions are more powerful than any answers you may have envisioned, and even the village idiot has questions you cannot answer."

"I do not understand," Kimrey said.

"When you have grown in reason, you will see that the best answers are often well-stated questions. When your reason has developed sufficiently, you may be able to pose the questions necessary to motivate change."

"What do you mean, Dunston?" Kimrey asked, more confused than ever.

"Making changes is rarely as effective as simply asking the right questions. What kinds of questions will you ask to expose the dishonesty in our politics? What kinds of questions will you ask to reveal the injustice in our laws? What kinds of question will you ask to stop the greed in our business dealings? Posing those kinds of questions will identify the real problems and the best answers will surface by themselves."

Kimrey was fascinated. Already, he was seeing things from a different point of view. "I have been taught many things, Dunston," he said. "My head is filled with facts and figures, history and current affairs, business and politics, but I am just now beginning to understand the value of my learning."

"Knowledge is a dangerous thing without reason, but one cannot apply reason to what one does not know," Dunston said as he stood. "I must go now, but I leave you with one last thought--reason shall lead you toward wisdom, for one cannot be wise about what cannot be reasoned, but all these things are vain without action."

Kimrey stood and straightened himself before his mentor. "I have much to learn from you, Dunston, and I shall try to be a willing charge."

And Kimrey was indeed a willing charge. He found serving in the Gallery to be considerably more interesting and challenging than he had envisioned.

During the next four years, Dunston became Kimrey's companion, advisor, teacher, and friend, and Kimrey developed a great respect for Dunston, for he saw that his mentor's experiences were vast, his insights keen, his compassion generous. Kimrey had always trusted Dunston with his secrets, his vulnerabilities, his insecurities, but now their relationship was even closer.

And Dunston held his charge in high regard as well. As each grew in understanding, respect and appreciation of the other, a fondness and fast friendship developed between them.

The winter of his twentieth year was also the year of the Star. Kimrey had reached the end of his apprenticeship with Dunston, and it was a sad time for both of them when they parted.

"If the Star does not destroy us, I shall assume my responsibility of governing Malthus with the coming of the spring," Kimrey began.

"And do you believe yourself equal to such duty?" Dunston asked.

"You have taught me well that I do not have the answers," Kimrey replied. "I am aware that I know only a little and I fear the loss of your guidance."

"No mentor can lead his charge beyond his own level of understanding," replied Dunston. "You have followed me as far as I can lead you. Use the crystal and summon the Guide when you know it is time for you to go higher."

Kimrey nodded. "Dunston, do you believe that it is I who will become the Keeper of the Trees?"

"Your mother believes it so," Dunston replied.

"But what do *you* believe?" Kimrey asked pointedly.

"If I do not believe that you are the chosen one, would it make it less so?"

"No," Kimrey said. "It would not change the truth, but I *would* like to know what you believe."

Dunston took a moment to consider his reply. "I do believe that you are not wholly of this world," he finally replied. "It is easy to see that this realm is alien to you. It requires no wisdom to understand that you do not belong here. I believe that you are a spiritual being struggling to understand a material world."

Kimrey looked into Dunston's eyes for a very long time. "I have always felt that I did not belong," he finally said. "Perhaps someday I will have the wisdom to know my place."

After a restless night Kimrey arose at dawn and ascended the Promontory Point to be alone in his wonder. In his desire to go beyond his own understanding, Kimrey took the crystal from around his neck and held it high. Suddenly, a dark figure wearing a brown hooded robe and carrying a crooked staff appeared at the edge of the wood. As they slowly approached one another, their eyes met. "I have come to lead you to the Ascetic," the Guide said. "It is time for you to begin your journey into wisdom." The Guide turned and started up the path.

Kimrey followed silently as the Guide led him swiftly up the mountain.

By noonday Kimrey was face to face with the Ascetic for the first time. As he seated himself in the stump chair, he felt a sense of awe, but his desire to know of his destiny overshadowed his reverence. "I have been told that I am the one you prophesied would be the Keeper of the Trees," he began. "Is it so?"

The Ascetic chuckled. "And if I told you that it were so, how would it change the course of your life?"

"I can prepare myself to be the best I can be if I know what it is I am to be," Kimrey replied.

"If your goal is too vivid, you might set your vision too high and trip on the pebbles which lie at your feet."

"I do not understand," Kimrey said with a blank stare. "Did you not summon me here to guide me through my Time of Wisdom? Am I not here to partake of your insights?"

"My wisdom would do you no service," the Ascetic replied. "You must seek your own."

"And where does one seek wisdom?"

"It lies in foolishness," the Ascetic replied.

"What does foolishness have to do with wisdom?" Kimrey asked.

"You shall see, Kimrey. As your experiences replace your innocence, foolishness shall provide you with the wisdom you need."

"But I know many who call themselves wise, and they do not appear to be foolish."

"Those who believe they have found wisdom never will," the Ascetic replied, "for they believe themselves too wise to be foolish. They have not yet found truth and integrity."

"But they are highly regarded, and people follow their teachings."

"Qualities that people admire are not always wise," the Ascetic replied.

"Then how will I know when I have found wisdom?" Kimrey asked.

"The Way says that no man has the wisdom to judge what is wise, for there are as many different kinds of wisdom as there are people. Each person's wisdom springs from unique experiences and what is wise for one may not be wise for another."

Kimrey frowned, rubbing his chin with his thumb and forefinger. "If wisdom lies only in each person's perception and interpretation, I can gain no wisdom from others."

"In finding The Way for yourself, it is best to stay out of The Way of others," the Ascetic replied.

"But if wisdom is unique to each individual, then is all wisdom not flawed?" Kimrey asked.

"Yes, my son, all wisdom is flawed," the Ascetic replied.

Kimrey was surprised by the Ascetic's reply. "If wisdom is flawed, then how can it be trusted?"

"You have just added to your wisdom," the Ascetic replied, "for you are beginning to learn that you know nothing. To know that you know nothing is to know that you have learned something."

"Are you saying that The Way to wisdom is to embrace ignorance?" Kimrey asked.

"Until ignorance is embraced, there is no thirst to know what it is you do not know, nor is there desire to understand what you do know."

"When will my purpose be revealed?" Kimrey asked.

"Your purpose is before you always," the Ascetic replied. "It is to seize opportunity."

"But how will I know which are the right opportunities?"

"It matters not what you choose so long as you pour your soul into it," the Ascetic replied. "Then, when your investment is complete, you will have the wisdom you seek. Wisdom does not come without experiencing the rawness of life."

"Are you saying that it is not necessary to know my purpose?"

"Each moment has its own purpose--to live to the fullest and to do what is put in front of you to do, even when you do not know the how or the why of it. It is The Way of faith."

"What does faith have to do with wisdom?"

"It is only men of faith who have wisdom," the Ascetic replied. "It is only they who know what life is all about. It is only they who see life as logical and reasonable."

Just then, the Guide appeared at Kimrey's shoulder. "Dusk approaches," he said.

Kimrey looked up at the deepening shadows on the ragged cliffs which surrounded them and knew that his visit had drawn to a close.

Chapter 27

A Change in Plans

With the spring, *The Adventurer* arrived at Aleph's Cove. Kimrey was about to leave his homeland for the first time and, despite all his mental preparation, he grew increasingly anxious as the moment of departure drew near. Reservations aside, he knew that he must fulfill his destiny and he set sail with Oberon at first light.

Kimrey spent much of the voyage in his cabin, alone with his thoughts. They were three days from port when he approached Oberon. "Will you tell me more of the land I am to rule?"

Oberon laughed. "You probably know more about Malthus than I. You have been better schooled in its history during the past six years than most Malthusians."

"It is true that I have learned well all that has been taught me of Malthus, but you live there; you have been their governor; you know about their day-to-day living, not just the things the politicians and scribes see and report."

Oberon was reluctant with his reply. "Yes," he said, "perhaps I do know things that some do not. I was with your father when he made his decision regarding their rule, and I have lived with the results of that decision ever since."

"What decisions did my father make?"

"He decided to decide nothing." Oberon replied.

"I do not understand."

"The Malthusians grew poor under Vistar's rule. With taxes high, and the commodities pool taking much and returning little, they barely sustain themselves."

"Does their tax money not purchase benefits from the government?"

"Only 20 percent goes to the welfare of the country, and that barely provides for the operation of the schools and the orphanages and the maintaining of the roads and water systems. Little is left for the services other governments provide."

"But what happens to the other 80 percent?"

Oberon was surprised at his question. "I guess I thought you knew," he replied reluctantly. "The 40 percent that once went to Vistar now goes to your father. The other 40 percent goes to the Malthusian politicians."

Kimrey felt like he had been hit in the stomach. He could not imagine his father, even at his worst, being so greedy that he would let such an injustice continue. "Do you mean that my father did nothing to distribute the wealth more fairly?"

"Perhaps he inherited not only Vistar's wealth, but his ways," Oberon said. "Long ago, your father made a vow to exact revenge on Malthus if it took the rest of his days. When he assumed the Monarchy, his opportunity was granted and he never had to lift a finger. All he had to do was to leave things as they were."

"It is not right that they continue to suffer unjustly while Oxymora prospers from their sweat," Kimrey scowled.

"Especially since it was not the people who did the wrongs, but the politicians," Oberon added.

"Your job here must have been a difficult one indeed," Kimrey said.

"They know that I sympathize with their plight," Oberon said, "but they also know that I have been powerless in my attempts to invoke a change of heart in Buceph. That is the challenge that is being left to you, my young friend."

"Just exactly what *have* I inherited, Oberon?" Kimrey asked. "Tell me of its darkest side."

"Very well," Oberon said. "You will find old women begging on the streets, young ones prostituting themselves, and hungry children stealing food from the market. The Seeds of Nod possess the minds of many, crime is ever-present, and degradation whispers at all levels of society. There is little enforcement of the laws and crime is rampant, though it is also well-hidden and covert."

"And it's brightest?"

"Most of the citizens here follow The Way. They have enough and are happy with their lives. Their needs are met and their wants have shrunk to match their possibilities."

"And what do they think of my father?"

"I"m afraid there is much fun poked at your father," Oberon replied.

"Humor often reveals cruel truths," Kimrey said. Both were silent for a time then Kimrey spoke again. "I need some time, Oberon. I need for you to carry on for a while longer until I have had time to see Malthus as the people see it. I must live among them so that I might know their hearts."

"But Kimrey, there are people here who know you," Oberon protested. "The diplomats have seen you in the gallery."

"Come now, Oberon, only a few of the high-level politicians have ever seen me. Do you really believe that I will bump into a diplomat while living among the commoners?"

"But everyone knows you are coming," Oberon said.

"Tell them you found me ill when you reached Oxymora," Kimrey pleaded. "Tell them I cannot make the trip until mid-summer."

Oberon stroked his beard but did not reply.

"Are you willing to help me?" Kimrey insisted.

"Very well," Oberon conceded reluctantly. "I shall hold my position until mid-summer, but not beyond that."

Chapter 28

Among the People

It was well past midnight when *The Adventurer* docked. Oberon quietly escorted Kimrey through the dark, empty streets to a local boarding house. He led Kimrey to the door, then, not wishing to be seen of anyone, said goodbye.

Kimrey settled into his meager room and slept soundly until the morning sun was high. He could hear the marketplace teeming with activity, as people from far and wide came to purchase and trade. The smell of tents and animals, the jingle of bells and trinkets amid the chatter, the rich textures of the ripe vegetables--these sights and sounds and smells reminded Kimrey of his boyhood in Trada.

He jumped from his bed, excited to be alive. As he dressed, he realized that his fine garments would be quite out of place. At the marketplace, he purchased a worker's frock and sandals then quickly returned to his room, dressed and put away his too-fine garments.

He took his breakfast at the boarding house. Fresh eggs, fresh-baked bread, and cold goats milk--just what his mother would have prepared. Having eaten his fill, he strolled back to the marketplace and wandered among the merchants and buyers, surprised at how much he felt at home.

He took his lunch at the nearby pub and his dinner back at the rooming house before retiring. He had successfully blended in with the crowd and was delighted with his new identity.

Lying there in the darkness, he listened to the laughter coming from the pub where he had lunched, and he thirsted to know more about them. What better place than the local pub to have a glimpse of the people? He dressed and headed toward the merriment.

Once inside, he ordered an ale and sat in the corner near the door. Two old men sat at the table next to him, and he could not help overhearing.

". . .but I am about to lose my farm," the first was saying. "The money I had for taxes went to the physician to care for my daughter. If I cannot meet my tax by the new moon, I shall lose everything."

"I would help, but all our surplus has already gone to the commodities pool," replied his friend. "What are you to do?"

"Perhaps I will go to Oxymora and join the ranks of the beggars on the palace steps at Bonaventure," the first man replied. "Buceph is known to throw money each day to those in need."

"It is true that many a beggar in Bonaventure lives better than the hard working people of Malthus, but surely you would never beg."

"Begging costs but little when you have lost everything of value," the first man said. "I cannot fill the bellies of my children with pride."

"I fear that our beloved Malthus is running headlong into its demise," said his friend. "Between taxes and the socialized commodities pool, there is little incentive to produce. It will just be taken away."

"Perhaps Kimrey will relieve our plight," the first man said.

"Kimrey will do no more than his father has done. He will be like Oberon--a pawn for Buceph. He will sit there in the Palace on the Mount, taking from his sheep, feeding them too seldom and sheering them too often. And when told that the flock grows hungry from lack and weak from cold, he will reply as his father replied: 'Who cares, so long as there is wool!'"

In those few short minutes, Kimrey's glimmer of hope was drowned in a wave of shame. He ordered more ale and drank quickly, and then more, and soon his queasiness melted into a black velvet blanket of numbness. It was pleasant, he thought, to just stop feeling.

Kimrey winced as the sun on his face snapped him to consciousness. As he slowly opened his eyes and began to focus, he was gripped with the most wrenching nausea he had yet experienced in his young life. His head was pounding, his muscles were sore, he had a terrible thirst.

Suddenly, he bolted upright, startled by a female voice. "Still alive I see. Bet your head is about to come apart."

Glancing quickly around the room, he realized that his surroundings were unfamiliar. He was in a strange bed, in a strange room, and he had no recollection of how he might have gotten there.

He squinted toward the voice, but her face was shadowed by the brightly sunlit window behind her and he could not make out her features. "Who are you? Where am I?" he asked sitting on the side of the bed.

"I am Samantha. I work at the pub," she said comfortingly. "You needed someone to take care of you last night. No one knew who you were or where you lived, so I brought you home with me."

"Weren't you afraid I might harm you?"

She laughed. "I have dealt with hundreds of men in their cups. After your tenth ale, you were in no shape to harm anyone but yourself."

"And what did I tell you of myself?" he asked suspiciously, not knowing whether he had revealed his identity.

"I know that you are new here, that you are a carpenter, and that you know nothing about holding your ale," she replied. "What is your name?"

"It is not important," he responded flatly. "I am no-one important; just a carpenter. I must go." He pulled himself to his feet and started toward the door, then paused. "Thank you for looking after me. I appreciate your kindness."

She nodded and smiled as he shuffled into the street, still inebriated. He saw the familiar marketplace just down the street and staggered toward his boarding house. Safe once more in his room, he nursed his pounding head and queasy stomach most of the day.

By evening, his appetite had returned and, despite his most embarrassing experience of the evening before, he was strangely drawn back to the pub. He entered the dimly lit tavern, looking about to see if he could spot Samantha.

"Hello, No Name," she called from across the crowded room. "I did not expect to see you back here quite so soon."

"Ale, please," he called as he seated himself at the same corner table.

Samantha smiled as she brought two bottles of the strong brew to his table. "I thought it would take at least a couple to get you feeling right again," she said.

He paid for the ale, giving Samantha a handsome tip, then sat forward in his chair, leaned his arm on the table and guzzled the first bottle. As he began to feel the warm glow he had first experienced the evening before, he sat back and sipped quietly on the second bottle and ordered a third.

During slow moments, Samantha would come to his table and sit with him and they talked. They talked of poverty and strife, of freedoms gained and hopes lost, and the longer they talked, the more Kimrey's shame rose.

By his seventh ale, his shame had once again given way to numbness. Samantha was busy with a new group of customers who had just arrived, and he sat quietly, alone in his mind, and drank himself into oblivion once more.

He awoke the next morning in his own room, though he had no recollection of returning home, nor did he have any recollection of most of the evening. Once again, Samantha was there. "I know, I know," he said, sitting up on the side of the bed. "I have not yet learned to take my ale. It takes me. Did I do or say anything out of line?"

"You were a perfect gentleman; something we will have to work on," Samantha replied with a giggle.

"I appreciate your taking care of me again, but why did you bother?"

"I guess I just feel sorry for you," she replied. "You need someone. You are the only one who comes to the pub alone and remains alone all the evening. You look terribly lonely."

Kimrey looked at her inquisitively. Then he stood, crossed the room and seated himself at the table which occupied the center of his small room. He sat there for a long while, staring wanly out the window. Samantha set a bottle of ale before him along with a plate of warm cereal and bread. "Ale the morning after helps to get you through the pain," she said. "After you drink it, you will be able to eat."

Kimrey grimaced, but turned the bottle of ale to his lips with shaky hands and drank it all. She was right. He did feel better, and his appetite returned. He finished his cereal and a large piece of the bread and Samantha placed another ale before him, which he quickly downed.

The warm glow so recently discovered returned, and he felt once more at peace and at ease. The restless discontent he had felt since his childhood was being held at bay and he wished that the feeling could last forever.

By mid afternoon, with several more ales under his belt, he invited Samantha to his bed. It was his first experience with a woman and Samantha was gentle, encouraging and understanding as he fumbled his way through his first sexual encounter.

Afterward, he slept until past dark. When he awoke, Samantha was gone. Feeling more lonely than ever, he dressed and headed once more for the pub, but Samantha was not there. He returned to her flat, hoping to find her there, but the shutters were drawn and no light shown inside. He returned to the pub and sat quietly at his table near the door.

He sipped his ale and listened to the merriment, but as he focused more on the revelry he sensed a gnawing undercurrent of unrest and hopelessness. The more he listened, the clearer it became that Malthus had many problems. It was hardly the picture of prosperity and contentment his teachers had painted. It was equally clear that the blame for those problems rested squarely on his father's shoulders. He knew that the things he had heard the two old men saying were true--his father sat high in his palace above the pain of the conquered and gloated in his superiority.

Ending the evening early, he retired to his room. He longed for the warmth produced by the ale, but he knew that he could not fulfill his purpose by keeping himself comfortably numb. He resolved that he would not return to the pub. Alone once again with his shame, he wished he could be anyone else, anywhere else on earth, and he sobbed himself into a deep sleep.

When he awoke, the world looked somehow a little brighter. After all, if anyone was in a position to better Malthus, it was surely he.

He thought of Samantha, and wavered for a moment in his resolve of the night before, but rather than returning to the pub, he threw himself into studying every aspect of Malthusian society. His mission became his obsession.

Before the month was out, he was having no difficulty blending into the crowd, and he methodically explored each facet of Malthusian society. He journeyed through the countryside to observe the workings of the farms, he labored in the flint mines to understand their operations, and he quietly followed Oberon around Port City to understand the mechanics of foreign trade. He contemplated all that he saw, ever mindful of ways to improve the quality of life.

Chapter 29

A Matter of Duty

It was near the end of his third month in Malthus when Oberon arrived at the boarding house late one evening. "It is midsummer, Kimrey. I am launching *The Adventurer* for Oxymora and the people here expect that you will accompany me on my return."

"Very well," Kimrey replied. "It is my duty and I must assume it."

"And have you learned all you wanted to learn about Malthus?" Oberon asked.

"I have," Kimrey replied somberly.

"Then let us be on our way."

"I do not wish to see my father," Kimrey said.

"Nor do I wish him to know that I still hold your seat," Oberon said. "My stay on shore will be brief--a couple of days at the most. You can remain on *The Adventurer*."

The Adventurer docked as scheduled and Oberon set out to Bonaventure as planned. As soon as he was gone, Kimrey dashed to the Promontory Point. He urgently needed the Ascetic's guidance. Holding the crystal high in the air, he awaited the Guide.

Once in the Ascetic's presence, Kimrey began spilling his doubts. "I have lived with great shame all my life, and my shame has only deepened now that I have seen the things my father has wrought. It seems an injustice that the Prophecy was bestowed on the House of Aleph."

"Worthiness seldom accompanies duty," the Ascetic replied.

"But there must be many who are more worthy," Kimrey said. "Why would such a noble task be entrusted to such an unjust, immoral and greedy lineage?"

"If worthiness were measured by justice, morality and generosity then none would be worthy," the Ascetic replied, "for even those who possess these qualities are selfish and self-serving."

"What do you mean selfish and self-serving?" Kimrey asked.

"Do you not see followers of religion who are moral, just and generous?" the Ascetic asked.

"Yes, but they are so only because they believe it will earn them a higher reward in the Place of Eternal Comfort."

"My point exactly," the Ascetic said.

"But are they not better for their religion nonetheless?" Kimrey asked.

"It depends on whether their religion is used to set themselves apart from others," the Ascetic replied.

"Set them apart?" Kimrey asked.

"Are not those who use their religion to separate themselves from others the very same who define *sin* as *separation*?"

"But surely religion, even badly practiced, places those who follow it above liars and thieves," Kimrey said.

"Who is more worthy, Kimrey, the man who gives that he might earn a favorable position in the Place of Eternal Comfort, or the man who steals that his children might not go hungry?"

Kimrey sat staring at the fire for a long while. The Ascetic finally broke the silence. "Your thoughts are far away."

"I was just wondering what it is that I am destined to bring to the Malthusian people," Kimrey said.

"It has been left to you to bring them hope," the Ascetic replied. "There is nothing as healing as expectations of a better tomorrow."

"I fear that I know only despair. How can I give them hope, if I have none?"

"Without despair, there is no need for hope," the Ascetic replied. "They are inseparable."

"And without pain there is no need for change," Kimrey said, "but there are many who know pain and are not willing to change it."

"For some, the fear of change is greater than the pain of withering away," the Ascetic said, "but happiness cannot be achieved without change."

Kimrey stared out to sea. "That sort of change can be painful," he said.

"Change causes no pain--only resistance to it is painful," the Ascetic said.

With that, the Guide appeared at Kimrey's shoulder. "Oberon will be completing his business soon," The Guide said. "It is time for you to return to *The Adventurer.*"

Kimrey looked toward the Ascetic and the old man nodded, then offered one more piece of advice. "Use your head when dealing with yourself so you can use your heart in dealing with others. And never get so caught up in what is urgent that you forget what is important--that happiness is mostly a by-product of overcoming self a little more each day."

The Guide returned Kimrey to *The Adventurer* late that evening, and Oberon boarded a short time later. By midnight they had set sail for Malthus.

Chapter 30

Rebellion

When *The Adventurer* docked at Malthus, the members of the high court were on hand to greet their new Monarch. They were gracious in their welcome and held an elaborate feast in conjunction with Kimrey's inauguration ceremony.

At the conclusion of the ceremony, Kimrey was asked to address the court and, with Oberon by his side, he began. "Despite my heritage, I am now Malthusian, and I hope to behave so. Being the son of Buceph has brought me great shame, for my father has done nothing to encourage prosperity in this land. Like Vistar before him, he takes much and returns little, but all that is about to change."

There was a brief murmur of curiosity from the politicians, but Kimrey continued, undaunted. "From this day forward, Malthus shall pay no tax to Oxymora. Malthus shall henceforth benefit from what Malthus produces."

All eyes turned toward Oberon. "But what will Buceph do?" asked the High Magistrate. "He has long hated our land. Will he not exact revenge on us for taking our independence?"

Oberon looked directly at Kimrey, smiling as he spoke. "I know Buceph well and I believe that he will abide what Kimrey decrees. I do not believe that he will contradict or do harm to his son." He then turned back toward the crowd. "Your new Monarch will lead you well. Follow him."

Satisfied with Oberon's reassurance, they returned their attention to Kimrey. "Beginning this day," Kimrey said, "there will be other changes as well. The commodities pool shall be abolished. Each shall keep what each produces to have and to use or as value for trade."

162

Another murmur rumbled through the court, for the commodities pool had long provided the politicians with surpluses which they used for their own profit.

"Then there is the matter of your government," he continued. "It, too, takes much and returns little. Henceforth, the government shall take no more than 10 percent of taxes collected to administer its affairs. We shall return 90 percent to the people in services and benefits. We shall improve our schools, provide for the enforcement of our laws, and offer each community essential services required to maintain public dignity. We shall do all this while cutting in half the taxes taken from the people."

The court remained condescendingly attentive as Kimrey completed his outline for change and they applauded politely when he had finished.

As they descended the steps of the court, Jorrell, the High Magistrate, joined Oberon. "Such radical reforms being imposed in such a cursory manner!" he said. "The young one has much to learn of diplomacy."

"He is not seeking popularity," Oberon replied, "though I suspect that his reforms will be well received by the people."

"Seasoned diplomats are always wary of sudden upheavals," Jorrell said.

"Then why did you not express your concerns?" Oberon asked.

"This was not the time nor place to react. It will take time to evaluate these radical changes carefully and respond in appropriate measure."

"It seems to me that there is little to evaluate, for his resolve is firm," Oberon replied. "His idealism asserts that there is to be plenty for all and his realism sees that this can only be achieved if there is opulence for none."

"Taking wealth from the politicians is not a popular way to inspire confidence," Jorrell said.

"The politicians will live an acceptable life," Oberon replied. "You may not have the wealth you once enjoyed, but you will want for nothing. And after all, what alternative would you choose? Would you become a miner, a farmer, a craftsman? I think not, Magistrate. In time you will see that Kimrey's decisions are wise."

"We shall see," Jorrell said. "We shall see."

And so it was that Kimrey's reign got off to a rather shaky start, but by the time a year had passed, Kimrey had won the hearts of most Malthusians. The Oxymorans sold their copper to all lands in a free market, and at a fair price, and the Malthusians were still able to make handsome profits on their superior goods.

And Oberon had been right about Buceph. There were no reprisals for Malthus claiming its independence and Buceph did nothing to interfere with Kimrey's reign. Buceph, in fact, was a bit relieved that both lands had been set free of the struggle to control the copper.

The Malthusian politicians still complained among themselves about the loss of their ostentatious wealth, but they could hardly air their complaints and divulge their greed, for they still lived in far greater luxury than the average worker.

With the people set free of the tyranny which had burdened them so heavily, free enterprise emerged and they regained a sense of community. Oppression slowly gave way to prosperity and most importantly, Kimrey's actions had begun to return dignity to the Malthusian people. He had impacted their lives in a most positive way, and they considered him a man of integrity and selflessness. He walked among them, and they admired his courage and humility.

As the weight of ill-gotten gains began to lift from his shoulders, so Kimrey's shame began to lift. He settled into a purposeful life as Monarch and for the next twenty years, he ruled Malthus with justice and integrity.

Chapter 31

A Time to Return

It was the Year of the Star, and as winter approached, it made its appearance on the eastern horizon. It was gigantic--the size of the moon, but brighter, and rising in the sky like a great sun. Terror spread throughout the land. Everywhere, people were given to panic, bewilderment, and hopelessness. It was upon them.

Kimrey was sitting quietly in his chambers, gazing out his window toward the chaos in the streets. People were running and screaming and weeping. He glared at the Star. Surely we will not escape this thing this time, he thought.

Just then, Oberon burst into Kimrey's chambers. "You must return home, Kimrey. Your father is dead."

Kimrey hung his head for a brief moment. A tear rolled down his cheek. "How did he die?" he asked.

"He was old, Kimrey. He was tired, and it was time."

Kimrey nodded. "Inform the court that I shall be going to Oxymora. My duties here shall be turned over to their best judgment until my return."

Oberon nodded, turned and left the room. Kimrey packed a few belongings, met Oberon on the veranda, and silently followed him to *The Adventurer*. By midnight they were well under way.

Kimrey stayed in his cabin until he had gotten past the initial shock and grief of his father's death. For three days, he remained in his cabin. Then, on the fourth day, he emerged and sought out Oberon.

Oberon was at his usual post at the helm. "It is good to see you out in the sunlight," he said as Kimrey approached.

Kimrey wasted no time with amenities. His head was filled with questions. "What will happen now, Oberon?" he asked.

"You are now Oxymora's Monarch," Oberon replied. "It is time for you to complete the circle and return to your beginnings. It is time for you to return home."

"But Malthus is my home," Kimrey said. "I have given my all to Malthus and I live there without shame." He frowned and stared at the deck. "I will complete my father's business, but I shall not stay."

"But Kimrey!" Oberon implored. "You have inherited the Monarchy. You cannot just ignore it."

"I no longer have any attachment to Oxymora," Kimrey protested. "Oxymora knows me only as Buceph's rebel son who declared independence for Malthus."

Oberon chuckled. "You did create quite a stir here when you decreed that Malthus would no longer pay tax to Oxymora, and your father's failure to retaliate stirred them all the more. It was hardly in his character to ignore such an action."

"Why *did* he ignore my rebellion?" Kimrey asked.

"Perhaps he finally grew weary of conflict," Oberon replied, "or perhaps he wanted to avoid the same kind of rift with you that he had with his own father. Whatever his reasons, he lived out his life quietly governing the land he loved."

"Was he a good ruler, Oberon?"

"Only history will be the judge of that," Oberon replied. "He had very strong beliefs, much as you, and he shaped Oxymora according to his ideals, but neither he nor anyone else found much happiness in his world."

"Then I shall not wear his shame for failing to do wrong," Kimrey said. He returned to his cabin and stayed there for the remainder of the voyage.

As *The Adventurer* approached Aleph's Cove, Oberon knocked on Kimrey's cabin door to announce their arrival. As Kimrey stepped out on deck, he stared up at Mount Erudite. It was brightly lit by the Star, and his thoughts turned to the Prophecy--the thing he had blissfully ignored for so long. It came as no great surprise to him when he saw the Guide awaiting his arrival. "I must visit the Ascetic," he told Oberon. "I will meet you in Bonaventure tomorrow."

It was with little enthusiasm that Kimrey trudged up the mountain trail, but once in the presence of the old man, he relaxed a bit. He told the Ascetic of his achievements in Malthus and his father's death, and he also spoke of his lingering shame. "I am here to inherit the remainder of my birthright," he began, "and I am saddened at having to return to the place where my shame was born."

"Then seek humility, for shame cannot exist without pride," the Ascetic said. "A person who has no pride has no shame either."

"How can you say that I am prideful?" Kimrey asked indignantly. "I have given my all for Malthus. I have served them well."

"Pride often shows itself through drawing attention to humble deeds," the Ascetic said.

"But I have given all that is in me," Kimrey said. "Are you saying it is not enough?"

"You just admitted that shame is the thing that is in you. Did you give them your shame?"

"I only gave them the best part of me," Kimrey said defensively.

"It is only the gifts you receive that are worthy of being shared with others. When you give of your own resources, you give only doubt and confusion."

Kimrey paused. "I would rather be remembered for whatever I gave them than for the legacy my father left me."

The Ascetic raised an eyebrow and looked Kimrey in the eye. "Humility will bring you no glory here, so you may as well not take such great pride in it."

"It has nothing to do with pride," Kimrey protested. "It is just that I receive so much when I give."

"So, you believe that you are only selfish and do not see yourself as prideful," the Ascetic said. "Has it ever occurred to you that when you give only to receive joy, praise, or a sense of superiority, your gifts are for your pride?"

"I suppose I thought my gifts would help them somehow."

"It is not that they do not help," the Ascetic said. "All gifts are helpful, but do you ever give thought to what your gifts do to the receiver?"

Kimrey stared at his feet as he shuffled them in the dirt.

"When you value your giving more than the receiver values the gift, the gift becomes a burden. If you wish to be a giver, first see to it that your gift is of value to the one receiving it."

Kimrey continued to stare at the ground. "I suppose I believed that if I gave enough, I would be accepted."

"No doubt it was your way of feeling safe. People find it hard to attack one so generous, but to be worthy of giving, you must first learn to receive."

"I seldom feel worthy of the gifts others offer me," Kimrey said. "I do not receive them well."

"Gifts are not given because they are deserved," the Ascetic said. "A gift is something you probably do not deserve, for you have not earned it. Otherwise, it would not be a gift. It is not about being worthy of the gift, Kimrey, it is about being worthy as a receiver."

"My father knew a great deal about receiving," Kimrey said sarcastically, "but he gave nothing in return."

"Taking is not receiving," the Ascetic replied. "Artful receiving is being grateful enough to thank others for what you are given and humble enough to thank them for receiving from you. But your father did fulfill his purpose well, and it was much to his credit that he never found much to his credit."

"Surely you are not suggesting that my father was a humble man," Kimrey said sarcastically.

The Ascetic shot a questioning glance toward Kimrey. "And just what do you know of humility?" he asked.

"I know that it is about putting others first," Kimrey replied.

"Then it must be very difficult for humble people to form a line," the Ascetic said with a chuckle. "That is not humility, Kimrey. Humility is remembering who you are, where you came from and what you made of yourself. It is glimpsing yourself as you really are. It is the ability to honestly see yourself and your relationship to the world around you. It is never lying about yourself and being very careful with the truth about others. It is pride that has lost itself in its own insignificance."

Kimrey stared out to the open sea. "Why is it that I must seek what I do not desire, Ascetic?"

"So that you will not become so pleased with yourself that you treat others carelessly," the Ascetic replied.

Chapter 32

Betrayed in Malthus

A month passed, and Kimrey tried to find enthusiasm for his position as Monarch of Oxymora, but his heart remained in Malthus. Here he faced new problems which demanded more than old solutions. To make matters worse, the heightened anxiety over the encroaching Star had begun to interfere with the smooth operation of business and government. It was apparent to everyone that Kimrey was unequal to the task of governing this land. He could not keep his focus on matters at hand and his leadership quickly proved completely ineffectual.

But the Star did pass, though everyone believed it would be the last time it would spare them, and by the time the Feast of the Passing Star was held, Kimrey had reached a point of desperation. In the midst of the feast, Kimrey approached his former mentor. "Dunston," he began, "I know nothing of ruling a land which struggles against itself. Everything I believe is being challenged, everything I say is ignored or criticized by the Council, everything I do is undone."

"The people do not trust your intentions," Dunston said. "They see you only as the Malthusian ruler who took riches from them."

"But I took nothing that belonged to them," Kimrey protested. "I only kept what belonged to Malthus."

"That is the way you see it," Dunston replied, "but the people of Oxymora see it differently. They have not forgotten the brutalities they suffered. They have not forgotten the price they paid for their freedom.

They still believe they are due the spoils of victory. Your father gave them those spoils and you took them away."

Kimrey's shoulders drooped. He sighed deeply and hung his head. "Why can't people just live in peace and let others do the same? My father's actions brought me great shame, and I vowed that I would spend my life giving rather than taking."

"If you feel shame, let it be for your own deeds rather than your father's," Dunston said. "Have you not done the same things your father did? Did you not rebel against injustice in order to gain power?"

" But I tried to use my power for the good of the land I served."

"And did your father not do the same?"

"You have always shown me things I could not see," Kimrey said. "I vowed to be different from my father, just as he vowed to be different from his father. We are alike."

"Each generation repeats the mistakes but learns different lessons from them," Dunston said. "Nonetheless, when you do the same things, you get the same results."

Kimrey hesitated for a moment. "Dunston," he continued, "you have served as Chief of the Council for many years now. It is obvious to me that the people place great trust in you."

"Most believe I have served them well," Dunston replied.

"If I give you the authority, will you govern Oxymora?"

"And what do you plan to do, Kimrey?" Dunston asked.

"I plan to return to Malthus."

Dunston nodded in acknowledgment of his acceptance. "I would be honored to be Governor of Oxymora."

Kimrey breathed a sigh of relief. "Then see to it that a proclamation is drawn up promptly. I wish to leave by eventide tomorrow."

By late afternoon the following day, Dunston presented Kimrey with a parchment containing the proclamation. Kimrey gave it a cursory glance then quickly signed it and returned it to Dunston.

By evening, they had set sail for Malthus. As Kimrey lay in his cabin listening to the waves slosh gently by, he felt safe once more. Throughout the voyage, Kimrey became increasingly eager to return to his duties as Monarch of Malthus. When the port city came into view, he stood on the bow in childlike excitement.

"We will be docking around midnight," Oberon said, interrupting Kimrey's anticipation.

"I was just thinking how wonderful it will be when things get back to normal."

"You are Monarch over two lands now," Oberon said. "Things will never be as they were."

"But I have given my responsibilities in Oxymora to Dunston."

"I wish it were that simple," Oberon said. "You will still be held accountable for his decisions and actions. And what will you do when you must make decisions which affect both lands? Will you favor one at the expense of the other?"

Kimrey pondered Oberon's questions for a time. "What do you suppose The Life That Is does when seafarers pray for sunshine and growers pray for rain?" he asked with a chuckle.

Oberon laughed. "Unfortunately, the Life That Is does not deal with worldly matters. The question is, what will *you* do?"

By midnight, they had docked and made their way to the state house. When they entered the great hall, they were greeted by armed soldiers blocking their path with crossed lances.

"What's this?" Kimrey demanded. "We have not armed ourselves in more than twenty years. Who has put you up to this?"

The soldiers stood staunchly and did not reply. Just then a voice echoed down the darkened corridor. "Kimrey? Is that you?"

Kimrey and Oberon strained to see who was calling, but the shadows hid his face.

"Let them pass," the voice said, and the soldiers relaxed their guard as Jorrell moved into the light.

"Jorrell!" Kimrey said. "What are you doing here?"

"I have been chosen by the people to be the new Monarch of Malthus," Jorrell replied.

"*I* am the Monarch of Malthus!" Kimrey said firmly, as he squared his shoulders. "It is my birthright."

"It was you who gave us the right and the freedom to choose our own leaders," Jorrell said. "How can you blame us for exercising it?"

"But why?" Kimrey asked. "Have I not been a fair and just leader?"

"Yes! Yes! Of course you have, Kimrey!" Jorrell replied reassuringly. "But when you inherited the Monarchy of Oxymora, the Court had no idea

171

what your intentions were to be. After months passed without hearing from you, we believed that you might not be coming back."

"And so you elected a new Monarch just like that?"

"A government needs leadership, Kimrey," Jorrell replied. "We had none."

"And the soldiers?"

"The Court began to fear that this turn of events might threaten our land. We thought it best to guard ourselves carefully for a while until we learned how this change might affect our welfare."

"You did not trust me after all this time?"

"The people of Oxymora trusted you until you abandoned them for Malthus," Jorrell replied. "We trusted you until it appeared that you had abandoned us."

Kimrey stood motionless, expressionless, then he turned, pulled the hood of his robe over his head and walked past Oberon, out of the state house and into the darkness.

Crying, alone, he wandered the dark, empty streets. He crept quietly past the boarding house where he first stayed, he climbed the steps of the Court where he had been inaugurated, he stood in the eerie silence of the marketplace, and he reminisced about times gone by.

His thoughts turned to Samantha, the only one who had ever soothed his pain. Suddenly he found himself walking briskly past the marketplace through the streets toward the old pub. "Would it still be there? Would it be the same? Would Samantha. . . ?" He stopped dead in his tracks. "Of course not!" he thought. "Don't be foolish! Too many years; too many changes."

Nonetheless, he continued toward the pub. As he rounded the corner, the lights of the old pub brightened his face. Coming closer, he heard the familiar laughter and his stomach went queasy as he approached the door. He entered the dimly-lit room and he stood in the doorway, reminiscing. It was just as he remembered it. Even the faces looked the same.

"Hello, No Name," a voice called from across the room.

"Sam . . . Samantha!" he stammered. "What are you doing here?"

"Take that table there and I'll get you an ale," she said smiling as she pointed to the table where he first sat many years before. He seated himself, never taking his eyes from her and in a few moments, she approached his table with two bottles of ale and seated herself across from him.

"Samantha," he said endearingly. "Never in my wildest dreams would I have expected to see you here."

"Some things never change," Samantha said smiling.

"I suppose you know who I am by now," he said.

"I've known who you were all along," she replied.

"Then why did you let me continue my facade?"

"It was *your* facade," she replied, "and I assumed you had your reasons for wearing it. It was no business of mine."

"I have often regretted leaving without explanation," Kimrey said, hanging his head. "I just didn't know how to explain it to you. My duty demanded. . . ."

"I know, I know," Samantha replied with a chuckle. "I do not pretend to understand what your world is like, but I knew you had your duty. You owe me nothing."

Kimrey smiled, relieved that he need not offer more excuses. "And what about you?" he asked. "What have you done with your life since I saw you last? Surely you have not been here serving ale all this time."

"Hardly; though I may have been better off," she replied. "Until three years ago, I was married to a ship's captain. He sailed one of Oberon's ships. Ah, he was a handsome one! He wooed me and romanced me and swept me off my feet. Then he took me with him to Carpathia and to his children. The problem was, he also left me there with them while he roamed the seas ten months of every year."

"Why did you not leave him and return home?" Kimrey asked.

"My husband was highly respected in his community and I knew no one. I could hardly solicit the help of someone he knew to help me get away. And besides, I couldn't leave the children. I did grow to love them, you know."

"So you unwittingly lost your prime to motherhood and I lost mine to duty," Kimrey said. "Did you leave him after the children were grown?"

"I didn't have to," she replied. "He was killed when his ship went down in a storm off the coast of Carpathia."

"I remember that shipwreck," Kimrey said, nodding. "A load of copper was lost."

"He did leave me a handsome inheritance, though," she said. "I am quite well off, you know."

"Then what are you doing here serving ale?"

She tossed her head back and laughed. "I spent my happiest times here. This is what I most love to do. These are the people I love being with the most. Where else would I be? What else would I be doing?"

"I envy you, Samantha," Kimrey said. "I wish I had such freedoms."

"And what prevents you from having them?" she asked. "Is it your duty?"

Kimrey chuckled. "My position here in Malthus has just been stripped from me. I am no longer Monarch. I no longer know what my duty is."

"Perhaps it is to enjoy life."

"Another ale, then!" he said, grasping his chalice and holding it high.

Morning came, and Kimrey once again found himself in a strange bed, in a strange room, with no recollection of the remainder of the night before. And again, Samantha was there. Dear Samantha. What would he do without her? She was the only one who had ever been able to take his pain away, and she was more than willing to see to it that Kimrey enjoyed himself to the fullest. It was she who led him to the pleasures of wine and wenches; it was she who introduced him to the Seeds of Nod.

For three months, Kimrey and Samantha spent their days behind closed shutters in Samantha's flat. There was ale to soften the stark morning light and rum to brighten the afternoon. Their evenings were filled with revelry at the pub and the Seeds of Nod enfolded them in a blanket of velvet darkness each night. How he welcomed the comforting numbness! For twenty years, Kimrey had denied himself pleasures; for twenty years, his life had belonged to someone else. So much responsibility, so much shame, so much sacrifice--so much to forget! Killing the pain was all that mattered.

In time, Kimrey's debauchery gave way to sickness--terrible sickness. The Seeds of Nod took him near to death and with his return to life came retching and gagging, cramping and shaking, and weakness from days without food.

Eventually, even Samantha could no longer endure his pleas, his insults, his stench, and she threw him into the streets.

Chapter 33

Betrayed in Oxymora

Kimrey squinted, trying to focus his eyes on the figure standing over him calling his name. "I see you are still alive," the booming voice pounded on his ears.

"Oh, hello, Oberon," Kimrey mumbled as he struggled to get to his feet, then he sat back, too weak to stand. "Where am I?"

"In the alley behind the marketplace," Oberon replied as he helped him to his feet. "Come, we'll get you cleaned up and get some food in you."

Kimrey stood there, swaying to maintain his shaky balance. "An ale is what I need," he said.

"You've had enough ale for a while, my friend. There are things you must attend to in Oxymora."

"Why should I care what happens in Oxymora?" Kimrey asked belligerently.

Oberon threw his arm around Kimrey's shoulder and guided him toward the street. "Come with me to my estate and I shall tell you."

Kimrey did not have the strength to resist. He tried to remember the last time he had eaten, but he could not. It took an enormous effort for Kimrey to bathe and dress himself in clean robes, but he somehow managed, then virtually vibrated down the stairs to the dining room. Oberon was already seated and hot food was waiting on the table. Kimrey tried to eat, but cold milk was the only thing he could force down his throat. "I need some ale lest I die," Kimrey pleaded, his hands trembling so badly he could scarcely hold his cup.

"Have you no shame, Kimrey?" Oberon asked.

"Have I no shame!" Kimrey snapped angrily. "Shame, my friend, is the one thing that I have in abundance."

"There will be no ale," Oberon replied firmly.

"Then get on with it so I can get back to my oblivion."

"Very well then," Oberon said. "Dunston is making radical reforms in Oxymora. He has raised taxes and taken away free enterprise. He has taken over the mines and controls trade and the market. All production now goes to the government and he has formed a powerful militia to enforce his proclamations."

"I'm sure Dunston has his reasons for doing what he is doing," Kimrey said, discounting the seriousness of the issue. "He would never take actions which would harm Oxymora or threaten the fulfillment of the Prophecy."

"He is not only taking such actions, he is blaming them on you, Kimrey," Oberon said. "He has made public pronouncements denying responsibility for the very things he is creating. He is saying that all is being done at your bidding."

"Surely the Council of Elders or the Priests will intercede before the situation turns too grave."

"They are as convinced as everyone else that your loyalty lies with Malthus," Oberon said. "What reason would they have not to believe him?"

"If all you say is true, he will soon have us at war," Kimrey said.

"And you will be to blame," Oberon added.

"But why would Dunston do such things? He has always fought for Oxymora's freedoms and he has done so in the name of the Prophecy."

"It is his revenge, Kimrey," Oberon said. "Many years ago, when you were but a lad, Buceph and Dunston had sharp disagreements. Your father said things to him--hurtful things that Dunston never forgave or forgot. He has carried this hurt with him all this time."

"And so he is making me his scapegoat to get back at my father?"

"It is not just that," Oberon continued. "Dunston also carries strong sense of entitlement. He felt that he was never given his due, and now that his years are short, he has no intention of dying a pauper. I suppose he believes that if his reward is not to be granted to him, he has a right to take it."

"Then why did he not take it sooner?" Kimrey asked.

"He could hardly defy the lineage of the Monarchy," Oberon replied. "Everyone in Oxymora supported it and believed in it. So as long as the

House of Aleph remained in power, he had little choice but to acknowledge your title and position. But now, with Buceph gone and you conveniently out of the way, it has become an easy matter to prey on what the people fear--that the House of Aleph has betrayed Oxymora in favor of Malthus."

"I suppose it is a good thing that he does not know I have been deposed in Malthus," Kimrey said.

"But he does know," Oberon replied. "Samantha has. . . ."

"What do you know of Samantha?" Kimrey interrupted.

"I have known her for many years," Oberon replied. "She married one of the captains in my fleet."

"Yes I know, but. . . ."

"Kimrey," Oberon interrupted, "Samantha works for Dunston. She went to Oxymora after her husband died. She had a substantial widow's inheritance and consorted with the top of Oxymoran society. That is how she met Dunston. Unfortunately, her opulent lifestyle rapidly depleted her resources. She lived beyond her means and her neediness soon became an embarrassment."

"What has that to do with me?" Kimrey asked impatiently.

"When Dunston discovered that she had a brief fling with you, he offered her substantial riches to return to Malthus and keep you out of the way."

"Samantha has betrayed me as well?"

"You would be surprised at the principles some people will compromise when faced with losing face."

Kimrey hung his head, his shoulders slumped, his arms dropped to his side. "She knew my weaknesses and used them against me."

"They have all used you for their own selfish gains," Oberon said, "and there are plots to overthrow your Monarchy even as we speak."

Kimrey put his head in his hands as tears began streaming down his cheeks. "He was my mentor," he sobbed. "She was my friend." His sobbing continued for several minutes more, then he straightened himself, wiped his cheeks and cleared his throat. "What am I to do, Oberon? There is nothing left. I have become an outcast from two lands who welcome outcasts."

"As strange as this may sound coming from me, Kimrey, there is only one thing which carries any import now. You must fulfill the Prophecy. You and the Prophecy are the only remaining hope for us all."

Kimrey's head jerked up in surprise. "Has madness seized you, Oberon? I thought you far too temporal to concern yourself with such matters."

"It matters not what has seized me," Oberon replied.

"You have talked with the Ascetic, haven't you?"

Oberon's admission lay in his silence.

"Very well," Kimrey conceded, "take me to Oxymora."

Chapter 34

Outcast by Outcasts

Kimrey spent most of the voyage regaining his strength. The ravages he had inflicted upon himself had left scars, but by the time they reached Oxymora he was strong and alert.

As Oberon and his crew moored *The Adventurer* in Aleph's Cove, Kimrey was clinging to the crystal, holding it tightly to his chest in anticipation of raising it high to summon the Guide the moment they arrived. But he did not need to--the Guide was waiting on the Promontory Point as they disembarked. Oberon nodded his encouragement and Kimrey followed the Guide dutifully.

As he approached the Ascetic's cave, his breathing quickened and his heart pounded. He tried to analyze his brimming emotions, but utter confusion ruled them all. He could no longer separate his hurt, indignity, and frustration from his shame, sorrow, and regrets.

Seating himself in the old stump chair, Kimrey began. "I come to you in shame, Ascetic, for I have lost everything."

"You have lost only riches and position," the Ascetic said. "It is not until you lose *truth* and *purpose* that you lose all."

"Even if I knew truth and had a purpose, what value would it be to me?" Kimrey asked. "Would it stop my pain?"

"Your pain comes from knowing too much truth and having too high a purpose, and then expecting the same from others," the Ascetic replied.

"I have suffered deep hurts at the hands of others," Kimrey said. "I trusted those close to me and they betrayed me."

"You gave those close to you responsibilities that belonged to you then blamed them for assuming those responsibilities."

"I never wanted them in the first place. They came with my heritage."

"And do you still find your heritage unworthy of you?"

"It is my heritage which has always brought me shame," Kimrey said. "That is why I have tried so hard to do things differently."

"Doing things differently is The Way. Each generation strives for a higher purpose. If you are still doing things the way the last generation did them, you are probably doing them badly."

"But I did them badly anyway," Kimrey said. "My good deeds were to prove myself too worthy for shame; my bad ones to prove myself too evil to carry it. I was foolish enough to think myself equal to any good deed, then found no bad deed beneath me."

"And what did you discover, Kimrey?" the Ascetic asked.

"I found it no better to do the right thing for the wrong reason than the wrong thing for the right reason. And no matter which I did, my shame remained."

"Shame is not about what you do--it is about what you believe you are," the Ascetic said. "It is the shadow of your pride."

"My shamelessness has left me with no pride."

"Some believe that shamelessness levels pride so that people may find humility. The Way says that finding humility levels pride, making it possible to become shameless."

Kimrey chuckled. "How ironic!" he said. "Oberon asked me if I had no shame just when I was the most filled with it. He found me in an alley, burned out from squandering my life on lusts and pleasures, taking comfort with whores, eating and drinking and drugging myself into daily oblivion. I had given myself over completely to the Seeds of Nod, but even that no longer took away my hurt. The terrors had hit me and I was begging for ale."

"Many die trying to kill their shame," the Ascetic said.

"Is that to be my fate? Must I succumb to it?"

"If you do not value the truth you have found over the damage you have done, then you are already dead."

"Do you not judge me for my misdeeds?"

"It is not mine to judge," the Ascetic replied. "When a person finds truth and purpose, the means by which they find them is of no consequence to me."

"But surely the Keeper of the Trees must be a man of integrity, someone worthy of the honor."

"The Trees do not consider the worthiness of those who bring them water," the Ascetic said, "and when they bear their fruit, they do not consider the worthiness of those who eat it."

"When will the mystery of the Trees be revealed to me, Ascetic? When will I know what I am to do as their keeper?"

"I shall reveal it to you now, but that does not mean that you will understand it," the Ascetic replied. "The Trees are Knowledge and Life; their Keeper, Truth and Purpose."

Kimrey was quiet for a long while. The Ascetic was right--he didn't understand it. "Can you tell me more?" he asked.

"There is no more to tell," the Ascetic replied.

Kimrey had no choice but to accept the Ascetic's answer. He paused, gathering his thoughts. "Oberon told me that I must concentrate on fulfilling the Prophecy--that it is the remaining hope for us all."

"Yes? Go on," the Ascetic urged.

"It's just that Oberon has never concerned himself with such things. What has happened to him?"

"Perhaps he is concerned about the legacy he will leave to you."

"Leave to me?" Kimrey asked with surprise. "Why would Oberon leave anything to me?"

"If you insist on judging your heritage, at least you should know what you are judging," the Ascetic replied. "You see, Kimrey, your mother is Oberon's daughter. Your heritage is as much from the House of Oberon as from the House of Aleph."

Kimrey was stunned. Scraps of his family history flashed through his mind. "Of course!" he thought. "It was Oberon who brought Beth to Judith and Rowland. . . ."

"Now I suppose you will have to judge which legacy brings you pride and which brings you shame," the Ascetic said, "and how much of each your ancestry must bear."

Kimrey shook his head. "I have learned one thing this day, Ascetic. I know that there is much I do not know, and I do not know what I do not know."

"Then you are ready for your victory," the Ascetic said. "Go into the Dark Forest alone and face what you find there. Success will follow."

Chapter 35

The Dove

Kimrey left the Ascetic and walked directly into the Dark Forest. He did not stop until he was deep into the wood where the daylight grew dim. Sitting beneath a tree, he watched the waning light fade to black. He made a bed of leaves and lay himself down. Sleep was long in coming but finally he did sleep, and a cloud appeared, and from the cloud emerged a dove. "I am The Life That Is, and I come to you as the spirit of love," said the dove.

Kimrey squeezed his eyes shut for a moment then opened them again, but the dove was still there. "Very, well," he finally said, "if you are the spirit of love, then why did you not come to me when I was all alone and needed you most?"

"I have never left you," replied the dove, "and you were never less alone than when you were all alone. You simply did not choose my comfort."

"I sought my comfort elsewhere and it led me only to sorrow," Kimrey said, hanging his head in shame.

"Then let your sorrow rejoice, for pain is as much a part of living as is joy, and one cannot be realized without the other."

A tear spilled from Kimrey's eye and down his cheek. "I am certain I shall have many days of contrition for my deeds before forgiveness comes."

"Penance is for those whose fear of me is greater than their love of people. Choose it, if you must, to absolve your guilt, but forgiveness does not come because you experience enough pain--it comes because you experience enough love, and love does not wait for anything."

"Do you not condemn me for my excesses?"

"What sense would it make for me to condemn what I have created?" asked the dove. "And besides, if I condemned those who indulge in excesses, would I not also have to condemn those who are excessive in their moderation? No, Kimrey, I do not condemn the sky for its storms, nor the rose for its thorns, nor the serpent for its venom. All these things are of The Life That Is."

"It seems to me that your love would be better spent on those who are pure," Kimrey said.

"Your purity does not force my love upon you nor does your arrogance deny it."

"But I have done nothing to deserve your love," Kimrey said.

"*You* do not control my love, *I* do," the dove replied, "and all your badness cannot kill it, nor can your goodness create it. My love is always there, and always freely given. It does not carry conditions or demands, for if it did, it would not be love."

"Then what is the purpose of religion? What is the purpose of prayer?" Kimrey asked.

"Is not your life your religion? Is each thought not prayer?"

"I suppose I thought there should be more," Kimrey said.

"Then pray each morning for love's will in your life and the strength to do love's bidding. And when you retire each night, pray that you are treated tomorrow the way you have treated everyone today. When you can pray these prayers in earnest, you will have all you will ever need."

Kimrey paused. "I suppose it would take a miracle to give me the kind of *faith* I need," he finally admitted.

"Miracles do not produce faith," the dove said. "Faith produces miracles, and they have been with you often."

"But I have seen no miracles," Kimrey said.

"Perhaps you did not see them because you were looking for magic, but I do not change the course of events--that would upset the natural balance of things."

Kimrey frowned, puzzled by the dove's reply. "But you must have breathed life back into me in that alley where Oberon found me."

"That is not the kind of miracle I perform," said the dove. "I did not tinker with nature to keep you from dying, but there *was* a miracle that day. The miracle happened when your desire to die went away. It was The Life

That Is in Oberon that loved you back to life. Miracles are most often a natural result of unselfish love."

Kimrey was silent for a time before he spoke. "Is it unselfish love that earns one entrance into the Place of Eternal Comfort?" he asked.

"The Place of Eternal Comfort is not some distant place for some future time. It is here and now," said the dove. "No matter where you are, it is always here; no matter when it is, it is always now. It is only in the *here* and *now* that the lamb sleeps under the lion's chin."

"What must I do from here?" Kimrey asked.

"The time has come to plant the Trees," the dove replied.

Kimrey wanted to ask about the Trees, but before he could, the dove returned to the cloud, and the cloud vanished.

Chapter 36

The Serpent Emerges

When Kimrey awoke, the Guide was sitting patiently by his side. Kimrey rose without a word and followed him up the trail. There was a calm inside he had never before known. Perhaps it was the leveling of his pride, or his enlightened understanding of The Life That Is, or his shame removed--whatever the reason, the vision of the dove had freed him.

Half way up the mountain, Kimrey stopped and sat down in the tall grass. Overwhelmed by his release, he began to cry and continued sobbing from the depths of his being until he was empty. He wiped his eyes on his sleeve and the Guide was sitting by his side once more. They rose together and, side by side, they strolled up the mountain trail.

By mid-afternoon, they had arrived at the Ascetic's cave. Kimrey seated himself on the ground at the old man's feet. Neither of them spoke as they watched the sun make its trek across the sky. Dusk was settling over the mountain when Kimrey finally broke the silence. "The day is dying."

"It is The Way of all things," the Ascetic said. "The cycle of *birth, life, death, birth* may be seen in all things--plants and animals, governments and nations, civilizations and continents, planets and stars and universes. Even the seasons and the years and the centuries--all these things are born, live and die and something new takes their place. And there are larger cycles of birth and death which you cannot imagine--knowledge and ideas and beliefs."

"I have often wondered what lies beyond death," Kimrey said. "I suppose I fear that it will be nothing."

"If you truly believe that there is nothing after death, then you have nothing to fear," replied the Ascetic, "but your reason tells you that there is much beyond this paltry journey."

Kimrey paused and stirred the fire. "In my vision, the dove told me that it is time to plant the trees."

"And the time has come to entrust you with them and the secrets they hold," the Ascetic said.

"Then the time has come for our world to die?" Kimrey asked.

The Ascetic rose from his seat, turned and started toward the cave. "Come with me," he said.

Kimrey followed dutifully. In the darkness of the cave a warm glow emanated from the far corner. Moving closer, Kimrey had his first look at the two very small, very fragile-looking seedlings which rested in baskets. They were no more than knee-high but radiant with energy. An unfamiliar bright red fruit weighed-down slender branches, and emerald leaves radiated a silvery shine. "These are the Trees?" he asked, bending over to study them.

"These are the Trees," the Ascetic affirmed, "and they shall give to humankind everything we have learned of that which lies between birth and death, and of that which lies beyond."

"But they are so small!" Kimrey said.

"Do not underestimate their power, Kimrey. They offer nothing less than humankind's free will. It is your duty to guard and protect humankind's right to become the creator."

"And how will humankind receive the Trees?" Kimrey asked.

"Some will blame them for their duplicity, others will praise them for the power of choice they offer."

"I'm not sure I fully understand just what it is they *do* offer."

"Lean closer and listen to what they tell you."

Kimrey thought the Ascetic's suggestion ludicrous, but with a skeptical glance he stepped forward and leaned his ear down to the first tree.

"I am the Tree of Life," the Tree whispered with a low raspy voice. "Partake of me and you will see that all that is, is meant to be."

Kimrey looked at the Ascetic. The Ascetic nodded, and Kimrey reached out, plucked a piece of fruit and bit into it. At once, his being melted into the tree's being. In his trance he and the tree were as one, and the thoughts

The Keeper of the Trees

and feelings of the Tree of Life, the tree of experience, were made known to him:

> The deeper my roots the higher I reach,
> And the more I can see, the more I can teach
> You of visions that blind you
> To freedoms that bind you.
>
> My branches reach out to those who are lost.
> Through cold and rain and wind-tossed
> Sea, they wave to and fro,
> But they must be pruned in order to grow.
>
> My leaves understand receiving to give;
> They know the purpose of dying to live.
> When they are attacked, they know to retreat;
> They live because they value defeat.
>
> I offer my fruit that all might drink
> Of life--to feel, and see, and think,
> And wonder of knowledge and reason and rhyme,
> Then to know that all things have purpose and time.

Before Kimrey could absorb what the first Tree had told him, the second Tree whispered in sweet angelic tones. "Partake of me and you will see duplicity that sets you free."

Kimrey, still entranced by the fruit of the first Tree, turned slowly and took a piece of fruit from the second Tree. He bit into fruit of this tree and his trance deepened, and at once his thoughts and feelings were at one with the Tree of Knowledge of Good and Evil. Said the tree:

> My roots have scars that you can feel,
> So you will know that you can heal.
> They cradle your shame, ignore your conceit;
> Their strength can bear your worst defeat.

My branches reach upward, firm and strong.
They uphold the right by bearing the wrong.
The smiles they show can bear your tears;
The faith they sew can bear your fears.

My leaves are wings that capture the wind,
But they know they will break if they do not bend.
Follow their course to learn how to lead,
And then, when you fail, you can stand to succeed.

My fruit bears joy to soften the sadness.
It offers the good to balance the badness.
The pleasure it gives shall bear your pain,
And all that you lose shall bear your gain.

Kimrey's face glowed with understanding. Slowly, he came out of the trance, straightened himself up and stepped back, in awe of what he had just experienced.

He became aware of the Ascetic's hand on his shoulder gently urging him backward, and his vision faded as they exited the cave. Returning to the fire, Kimrey sat himself down at the Ascetic's feet and the Ascetic offered him some warm tea. "Tell me of the new garden," Kimrey urged. "Will the Star not destroy all suitable places to plant the Trees?"

"It is the Star that will create the garden," the Ascetic replied. "The new land will rise from the sea west of Nod and it shall be called Eden. It shall be yours forever. It is there that you shall offer the Trees to humankind."

"Perhaps I will finally be valued for something of importance," Kimrey said with pride.

"No Kimrey," the Ascetic said, "you will not be valued. You will not be forgotten, but you will find no acclaim for your deeds. Humankind will not understand your gift for many millennia."

"Then how shall I be remembered?" Kimrey asked.

"Henceforth, from now until forever, you shall be known as the Serpent."

Kimrey's shoulders drooped, his body slumped, his stomach churned. He gazed disbelievingly into the Ascetic's eyes. "Is this my damnation?" he asked. "Is this my punishment for the life I have led?"

189

"You, too, misunderstand the Serpent, Kimrey, for the Serpent brings nothing less to humankind than the nourishment by which the spirit grows. The gift of the Serpent is the gift of free will. Without the Serpent and the Trees, there would be no choices, no mistakes, no challenges, and the spirit would not grow. The Trees offer humankind a chance to cease living in the pride and shame of being human. They offer humankind a chance to embrace its humanness, a chance to live and change and grow and become."

Kimrey was quiet for a time, staring at the ground. "Then I have but one more question, Ascetic. To what end do the Trees offer these things?"

"So people can discover and experience the perfect principle of unconditional love. The Trees offer welcome, so that all those outcast might come home. All who partakes of them shall come to understand the great principle of The Way--*know that love is all there is, and you will know all there is to know.*"

Kimrey stared out into space for several moments, taking the Ascetic's words to heart. "The Star is high on the horizon," he said. "It will soon be upon us. What will happen to you, Ascetic?"

"I never was and always will be, and you may summon me whenever you wish. The Guide shall never leave you."

"Will you be here on the mountain?"

The Ascetic chuckled. "This old mountain shall soon be but an island in the sea and I shall dwell here no more."

"Then where shall I look for you?" Kimrey asked.

"Where you have always found me--in The Life That Is in your mind and your spirit. Summon the Guide in your mind and I shall appear in your spirit. It is there that I have always been; it is there that I shall always be."

Kimrey paused, then continued. "Then has your journey here ended?"

"Until I return one day to experience the rawness of life once more," the Ascetic replied. "For now it is time for me to go back to the Ether and for you to sail away. *The Adventurer* will be awaiting you upon the tide, and Oberon shall deliver you to the new garden. The new garden is a haven for the lost, and it shall welcome you. It is there that you shall remain forever."

And so it was that Kimrey did sail away, and as he stood there on the bow of *The Adventurer*, feeling it bound rhythmically through the water, there was no fear, no anger, no shame. There was no more wondering, no more wishing, no more pleading. There was no more strife and no more pain, no more trying and no more failing. It was a perfect surrender and a perfect peace.

As they sailed westward past Nod toward the new land, the Star cut a blazing path across the sky directly over them, dropping a fiery rain as it flew by. When it struck on the distant horizon, it lit up the western sky with its blinding devastation.

As Eden rose from the sea before them a great rush of wind swept them swiftly toward their destination, and Kimrey remembered the Ascetic's promise--*success can only follow a victory*. Finally, he understood. *There will always be greater things than our selves to discover, but we must be greater than our selves to discover them. It is The Way of The Life That Is*.

To order additional copies of **The Keeper of the Trees**, complete the information below.

Ship to: (please print)

Name _____

Address _____

City, State, Zip _____

Day phone _____

_____ copies of *Keeper of the Trees* @ $10.00 each $ _____

Postage and handling @ $1.00 per book $ _____

New Mexico residents add 5% tax $ _____

Total amount enclosed $ _____

Make checks payable to **D. Rodney Blanks - CSS Publishing**

Send to: P.O. Box 779
Ruidoso Downs, NM 88346-0779

To order additional copies of **The Keeper of the Trees**, complete the information below.

Ship to: (please print)

Name _____

Address _____

City, State, Zip _____

Day phone _____

_____ copies of *Keeper of the Trees* @ $10.00 each $ _____

Postage and handling @ $1.00 per book $ _____

New Mexico residents add 5% tax $ _____

Total amount enclosed $ _____

Make checks payable to **D. Rodney Blanks - CSS Publishing**

Send to: P.O. Box 779
Ruidoso Downs, NM 88346-0779